# CORE SKILLS

## Houghton Mifflin Harcourt

# Math

## Grade 5

Copyright © 2014 by Houghton Mifflin Harcourt Publishing Company

Printed in the U.S.A.

ISBN 978-0-544-26823-4

2 3 4 5 6 7 8 9 10  0928  22 21 20 19 18 17 16 15 14

4500493590  A B C D E F G

# Core Skills Math

## GRADE 5

## Table of Contents

© Houghton Mifflin Harcourt Publishing Company

Table of Contents
Core Skills Math, Grade 5

Table of Contents
Core Skills Math, Grade 5

# Common Core State Standards for Mathematics Correlation Chart

## Operations and Algebraic Thinking

**Write and interpret numerical expressions.**

| 5.OA.1 | 16, 17, 18, 19 |
|---|---|
| 5.OA.2 | 25 |

**Analyze patterns and relationships.**

| 5.OA.3 | 26, 27, 74 |
| *Supporting Skills* | 28 |

## Number and Operations in Base Ten

**Understand the place value system.**

| 5.NBT.1 | 2, 3, 4, 5, 6, 13, 35 |
|---|---|
| 5.NBT.2 | 1, 14, 15, 76, 84 |
| 5.NBT.3 | |
|    5.NBT.3.a | 7, 8, 9, 10, 11, 12 |
|    5.NBT.3.b | 20, 21, 22 |
| 5.NBT.4 | 23, 24 |

**Perform operations with multi-digit whole numbers and with decimals to hundredths.**

| 5.NBT.5 | 36, 37, 38, 39, 40, 41, 42 |
|---|---|
| 5.NBT.6 | 50, 51, 52, 53, 54, 55, 56, 57, 58, 59, 60, 61, 62, 63, 64, 65, 66 |
| 5.NBT.7 | 29, 30, 31, 32, 33, 34, 77, 78, 79, 80, 81, 82, 83, 85, 86, 87, 88 |

## Number and Operations—Fractions

**Use equivalent fractions as a strategy to add and subtract fractions.**

| 5.NF.1 | 96, 97, 98, 99, 100, 101, 102, 103, 104, 105, 106, 107 |
| *Supporting Skills* | 89 |
| 5.NF.2 | 108, 109 |

**Apply and extend previous understandings of multiplication and division to multiply and divide fractions.**

| 5.NF.3 | 90, 91, 92, 93 |
|---|---|
| 5.NF.4 | |
|    5.NF.4.a | 110, 111, 113, 114, 115, 117, 119 |
|    5.NF.4.b | 112, 118 |

| 5.NF.5 | |
|---|---|
| 5.NF.5.a | 94, 95 |
| 5.NF.5.b | 116, 120 |
| 5.NF.6 | 122, 123, 124, 131 |
| 5.NF.7 | |
| 5.NF.7.a | 127, 128 |
| 5.NF.7.b | 121, 125, 129 |
| 5.NF.7.c | 126, 130 |

## Measurement and Data

**Convert like measurement units within a given measurement system.**

| 5.MD.1 | 132, 133, 134, 135, 137, 139, 140, 141 |
|---|---|
| *Supporting Skills* | 138 |

**Represent and interpret data.**

| 5.MD.2 | 75 |
|---|---|
| *Supporting Skills* | 136 |

**Geometric measurement: understand concepts of area and relate area to multiplication and to addition.**

| 5.MD.3 | |
|---|---|
| 5.MD.3.a | 144 |
| 5.MD.3.b | 142, 143 |
| 5.MD.4 | 145, 149 |
| 5.MD.5 | |
| 5.MD.5.a | 146 |
| 5.MD.5.b | 147, 148, 150, 151, 152 |
| 5.MD.5.c | 153 |

## Geometry

**Graph points on the coordinate plane to solve real-world and mathematical problems.**

| 5.G.1 | 67, 68, 69, 70 |
|---|---|
| 5.G.2 | 71, 72, 73 |

**Classify two-dimensional figures into categories based on their properties.**

| 5.G.3 | 43, 44, 46, 49 |
|---|---|
| 5.G.4 | 47, 48 |
| *Supporting Skills* | 45 |

# Grouping Symbols

**Evaluate each expression. Perform the operation in the innermost set of grouping symbols first.**

**1.** $5 \times [(1 \quad 3) - (13 - 9)]$

_____

**2.** $30 - [(9 \times 2) - (3 \times 4)]$

_____

**3.** $36 \div [(14 - \quad - (10 - 7)]$

_____

**4.** $7 \times [(9 + 8) - (12 - 7)]$

_____

**5.** $[(25 - 11) + (15 \quad 9)] \div 5$

_____

**6.** $[(8 \times 9) - (6 \times 7)] - 15$

_____

**7.** $8 \times \{[(7 + 4) \times 2] - \quad 1 - 7) \times 4]\}$

_____

**8.** $\{[(8 - 3) \times 2] + [(5 \times 6) - 5]\} \div 5$

_____

## MIXED APPLICATIONS

**Use the information below for Exercises 9 and 10.**

> Joan has a cafe. Each day, she bakes 24 muffins. She gives away 3 and sells the rest. Each day, she also bakes 36 cupcakes. She gives away 4 and sells the rest.

**9.** Write an expression to represent the total number of muffins and cupcakes Joan sells in 5 days.

_____

**10.** Evaluate the expression to find the total number of muffins and cupcakes Joan sells in 5 days.

_____

# Order of Operations with Parentheses and Exponents

**Use mental math and the order of operations to find the value of the expression.**

**1.** $21 + 29 - 25 =$ _____

**2.** $36 \div 9 - 2 =$ _____

**3.** $48 \div (6 \times 2) =$ _____

**4.** $4 \times 3 + 2 - 7 =$ _____

**5.** $45 \div 15 + 2 \times 3 =$ _____

**Find the value of the expression. You may use a calculator.**

**6.** $18^2 - 30 \div 15 \times 9 =$ _____

**7.** $12.8 + 6 \times 3^2 - 4^3 =$ _____

**8.** $(54 - 3) \div 17 + 63 \div 3^2 =$ _____

**Rewrite each equation using parentheses to make the answer true.**

**9.** $3 \times 8 - 5 = 9$ _____

**10.** $20 + 12 \div 4 + 4 = 4$ _____

**11.** $15 - 3 \div 12 + 1 = 2$ _____

## MIXED APPLICATIONS

**12.** The members of the swimming team have the following heights: 183 cm, 157 cm, 165 cm, 146 cm, and 179 cm. Write and solve a number sentence that uses division by 5 to find the average (median) height of the team members.

_____

_____

**13.** The members of the basketball team ordered 5 tuna sandwiches at $3.99 each, 5 fish tacos at $2.75 each, 3 salads at $2.70 each, and 13 drinks at $0.89 each. Write a number sentence that could be used to find the total cost of the food.

_____

_____

# Order of Operations with Fractions

**Apply the Order of Operations to solve.**

**1.** $5 \times (2 + 7) =$ _____

**2.** $18 - (2 \times 6) =$ _____

**3.** $(9 - 3) \times 7 =$ _____

**4.** $25 \div (10 - 5) =$ _____

**5.** $4 \times 6 \div 3 =$ _____

**6.** $7 + 3 \times 9 =$ _____

**7.** $18 - 5 \times 3 =$ _____

**8.** $3 \times 7 + 12 \div 2 =$ _____

**9.** $36 \div 9 + 8 =$ _____

**10.** $8 + 8 \div 2 + 3 =$ _____

**11.** $12 \div 4 + 24 \div 8 =$ _____

**12.** $12 \times 3 - 4 =$ _____

**In Exercises 13–21, each expression contains a fraction. If necessary, simplify the numerator or denominator. Then apply the Order of Operations to solve.**

**13.** $\dfrac{14 + 4}{3} =$ _____

**14.** $\dfrac{8 + 4}{8 - 6} =$ _____

**15.** $\dfrac{4 \times 8}{2} =$ _____

**16.** $\dfrac{3 \times 4^2 + 8 - 6}{2} =$ _____

**17.** $\dfrac{18 - 3}{3} =$ _____

**18.** $\dfrac{6 \times 7 - 18}{6} =$ _____

**19.** $\dfrac{6 \times (63 - 43)}{10} =$ _____

**20.** $9^2 \times (14 \div 2) =$ _____

**21.** $\dfrac{4.2 + 3^2}{8.6 + 4.6} =$ _____

## MIXED APPLICATIONS

**For Exercises 22–23, write the expression. Then compute the answer.**

**22.** Add the product of four and two to three squared. Then subtract one.

_____

**23.** Find the difference between the product of six and three and three squared.

_____

## VISUAL THINKING

**24.** Arrange the numbers 1–9 on the triangle so that the sums of the four numbers shown on each side of the triangle are equal. Use each number once.

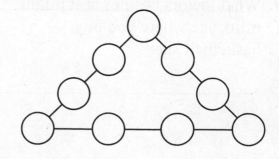

# Comparing Decimals

**Compare. Write < or >.**

**1.** 0.87 ◯ 0.78          **2.** 0.64 ◯ 0.93          **3.** 0.851 ◯ 0.85

**4.** 0.12 ◯ 0.21          **5.** 0.23 ◯ 0.32          **6.** 0.761 ◯ 0.176

**7.** 0.59 ◯ 0.63          **8.** 0.41 ◯ 0.21          **9.** 0.385 ◯ 0.583

**10.** 0.89 ◯ 0.98         **11.** 0.81 ◯ 0.19         **12.** 0.326 ◯ 0.246

**For Exercises 13–15 circle the number in which the digit 8 has the greater value.**

**13.** 0.68 or 6.85          **14.** 0.816 or 2.138          **15.** 0.381 or 0.948

## MIXED APPLICATIONS

**16.** Which fruit costs more, kiwi or oranges?

_____

**17.** Which items cost less than one dollar?

_____

| Prices of Groceries | |
|---|---|
| Kiwi fruit | $0.79 for 2 |
| Oranges | $0.95 for 2 |
| Apple cider | $1.99 per gal |
| Potatoes | $0.89 for 5 lb |

## EVERYDAY MATH CONNECTION

**18.** Which store charges the least for the basketball shoes?

_____

**19.** What factors besides cost might influence where you buy basketball shoes?

_____

| Prices – Same Basketball Shoes | |
|---|---|
| **Store** | **Price** |
| Ace Athletics | $51.95 |
| Like A Pro | $51.15 |
| Sports Mart | $51.29 |
| Fast Feet | $51.79 |

Name _____ Date _____

# Comparing Whole Numbers and Decimals

**Compare. Write < or >.**

1. 0.62 ◯ 0.56    **2.** 31.89 ◯ 3.18    **3.** 10.23 ◯ 1.28

**4.** 2.600 ◯ 2.006    **5.** 615.280 ◯ 651.208    **6.** 7.779 ◯ 7.797

**7.** 86.40 ◯ 86.34    **8.** 4.340 ◯ 44.034    **9.** 4,900.065 ◯ 4,900.650

**10.** 655.155 ◯ 655.515    **11.** 43.960 ◯ 43.906    **12.** 96.021 ◯ 96.201

**13.** 32.841 ◯ 328.410    **14.** 4.004 ◯ 4.008    **15.** 2.101 ◯ 2.110

**For Exercises 16–18 circle the number in which the digit 4 has the greater value.**

**16.** 32.841 or 328.410    **17.** 4.003 or 0.403    **18.** 5.034 or 1.048

## MIXED APPLICATIONS

19. Craig ran the race in 78.6 seconds. Mike ran the race in 76.9 seconds. Who ran the faster race? Explain.

_____

_____

20. The batting averages of four players are: 0.268, 0.280, 0.299, and 0.245. What decimal place do you need to compare to see which batting average is best? Explain.

_____

_____

## WRITER'S CORNER

21. Write and answer a problem that can be answered by comparing two decimal numbers.

_____

_____

# Comparing Decimals with Zeros

**Compare. Write <, > or =.**

**1.** 0.03 ◯ 0.32     **2.** 0.047 ◯ 0.47     **3.** 0.5 ◯ 0.500

**4.** 0.125 ◯ 0.13     **5.** 0.15 ◯ 0.115     **6.** 2.658 ◯ 2.60

**7.** 0.620 ◯ 0.62     **8.** 0.11 ◯ 0.110     **9.** 0.26 ◯ 0.3

**10.** 5.501 ◯ 0.56     **11.** 0.95 ◯ 0.905     **12.** 9.5 ◯ 9.50

**Circle the greater number.**

**13.** 0.25     0.3          **14.** 0.65     0.605          **15.** 3.008     3.080

**16.** 4.50     4.050          **17.** 0.78   0.789          **18.** 2.001     2.01

**Circle the smallest number.**

**19.** 67.5   0.675   65.07          **20.** 7.026   7.260   7.230          **21.** 0.34   0.034   0.304

---

## MIXED REVIEW

**22.** Use a basic fact and mental math to find the products.

$10 \times 7 =$ _____

$100 \times 7 =$ _____

$100 \times 70 =$ _____

**23.** Complete the pattern.

$4 \times 6 =$ _____

$4 \times 60 =$ _____

$4 \times 600 =$ _____

$4 \times 6,000 =$ _____

---

## NUMBER SENSE

**Compare. Write <, > or =.**

**24.** $30 \times 5$ ◯ $20 \times 9$          **25.** $45 \times 10$ ◯ $90 \times 5$

**26.** $40 \times 80$ ◯ $4 \times 800$          **27.** $20 \times 30$ ◯ $200 \times 300$

# Decimals: Estimation and Rounding

1. Use the number line to find which numbers in the box round to 4.0. Circle the numbers.

3.0        4.0        5.0        6.0

| 3.3 | 5.2 | 5.8 |
|-----|-----|-----|
| 5.9 | 5.5 | 3.7 |
| 3.8 | 4.1 | 4.6 |
| 4.2 | 3.1 | 4.4 |

**Round to the nearest whole number.**

2. 8.1 _____    3. 9.7 _____    4. 1.6 _____    5. 0.78 _____

6. 21.41 _____    7. 13.87 _____    8. 24.09 _____    9. 52.56 _____

---

## MIXED APPLICATIONS

**Use the map to answer Exercises 10–11.**

10. To the nearest kilometer, what is the shortest distance from Brookby to Ed's Peak?

_____

11. To the nearest kilometer, what is the distance from Naylor Bridge to Taylorville along the Wagman River Trail?

_____

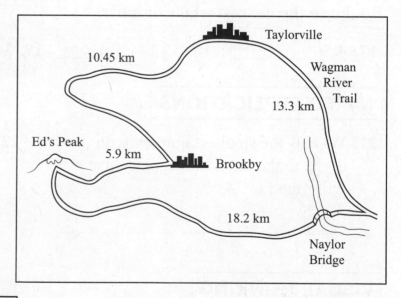

---

## LANGUAGE ARTS CONNECTION

12. Todd read these phrases in the newspaper. He knows that some of the numbers are exact but thinks others must be rounded. Circle any number that you think is most likely a rounded number.

14 honored at mayor's office        seating capacity 432        132,000 tickets sold

25.5 million voters        trail length 3.8 miles        length of movie 1 hr 57 min

**23**

Name _____ Date _____

# Rounding Decimals

**Round to the nearest tenth.**

**1.** 0.43 _____    **2.** 0.45 _____    **3.** 12.79 _____

**4.** 46.36 _____    **5.** 1,234.72 _____    **6.** 4,513.79 _____

**Round to the nearest hundredth.**

**7.** 0.123 _____    **8.** 0.148 _____    **9.** 3.547 _____

**10.** 85.612 _____    **11.** 175.431 _____    **12.** 78.465 _____

**Round to the nearest dollar.**

**13.** $4.57 _____    **14.** $15.19 _____    **15.** $123.79 _____    **16.** $56.82 _____

**Round to the nearest whole number.**

**17.** 4.56 _____    **18.** 12.14 _____    **19.** 34.72 _____    **20.** 67.88 _____

## MIXED APPLICATIONS

**21.** What is the smallest number with digits to the thousandths place that will round to 34.6?

_____

**22.** Jeff wants to buy a book that cost $12.25. He has no coins. What is the least number of dollars he must take to the store?

_____

## VISUAL THINKING

For Exercises 23–24, round the shaded area to the nearest tenth. For Exercises 25–26, round the shaded area to the nearest hundredth.

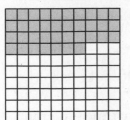  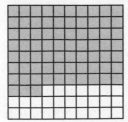  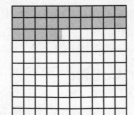  

**23.** _____    **24.** _____    **25.** _____    **26.** _____

Unit 2
Core Skills Math, Grade 5

# Numerical Expressions

**Write an expression to represent the words.**

**1.** Ethan collected 16 seashells. He lost 4 of them while walking home.

_____

**2.** Yasmine bought 4 bracelets. Each bracelet cost $3.

_____

**3.** Amani did 10 jumping jacks. Then she did 7 more.

_____

**4.** Darryl has a board that is 8 feet long. He cuts it into pieces that are each 2 feet long.

_____

**Write each numerical expression in words.**

**5.** $3 + (4 \times 12)$ _____

**6.** $36 \div 4$ _____

**7.** $24 - (6 + 3)$ _____

**Draw a line to match the expression with the words.**

**8.** Ray picked 30 apples and put them equally into 3 baskets. Then he ate two of the apples in a basket.

$(3 \times 2) \times 30$

**9.** Quinn had $30. She bought a notebook for $3 and a pack of pens for $2.

$(30 \div 3) - 2$

**10.** Colleen runs 3 miles twice a day for 30 days.

$30 - (3 + 2)$

---

## MIXED APPLICATIONS

**11.** Kylie has 14 polished stones. Her friend gives her 6 more stones. Write an expression to match the words.

_____

**12.** Rashad had 25 stamps. He shared them equally among himself and 4 friends. Then Rashad found 2 more stamps in his pocket. Write an expression to match the words.

_____

# Numerical Patterns

**Complete the rule that describes how one sequence is related to the other. Use the rule to find the unknown term.**

**1.** Multiply the number of laps by _____ to find the number of yards.

Think: The number of yards is how many times the number of laps?

| Swimmers | 1 | 2 | 3 | 4 |
|---|---|---|---|---|
| Number of Laps | 4 | 8 | 12 | 16 |
| Number of Yards | 200 | 400 | 600 | |

**2.** Multiply the number of pounds by _____ to find total cost.

| Boxes | 1 | 2 | 3 | 4 | 6 |
|---|---|---|---|---|---|
| Number of Pounds | 3 | 6 | 9 | 12 | 18 |
| Total Cost ($) | 12 | 24 | 36 | 48 | |

**3.** Multiply the number of hours by _____ to find the number of miles.

| Cars | 1 | 2 | 3 | 4 |
|---|---|---|---|---|
| Number of Hours | 2 | 4 | 6 | 8 |
| Number of Miles | 130 | 260 | 390 | |

**4.** Multiply the number of hours by _____ to find the amount earned.

| Days | 1 | 2 | 3 | 4 | 7 |
|---|---|---|---|---|---|
| Number of Hours | 8 | 16 | 24 | 32 | 56 |
| Amount Earned ($) | 96 | 192 | 288 | 384 | |

## MIXED APPLICATIONS

**5.** A map distance of 5 inches represents 200 miles of actual distance. Suppose the distance between two cities on the map is 7 inches. What is the actual distance between the two cities? Write the rule you used to find the actual distance.

_____

_____

_____

**6.** To make one costume, Rachel uses 6 yards of material and 3 yards of trim. Suppose she uses a total of 48 yards of material to make several costumes. How many yards of trim does she use? Write the rule you used to find the number of yards of trim.

_____

_____

_____

**26**

# Problem Solving

## FIND A RULE

**Write a rule and complete the table. Then answer the question.**

**1.** Faye buys 15 T-shirts, which are on sale for $3 each. How much money does Faye spend?

| Number of T-shirts | 1 | 2 | 3 | 5 | 10 | 15 |
|---|---|---|---|---|---|---|
| Amount Spent ($) | 3 | 6 | 9 | | | |

Possible rule:

_____

_____

The total amount Faye spends is _____.

**2.** The Gilman family joins a fitness center. They pay $35 per month. By the 12th month, how much money will the Gilman family have spent?

| Number of Months | 1 | 2 | 3 | 4 | 5 | 12 |
|---|---|---|---|---|---|---|
| Total Amount of Money Spent ($) | 35 | 70 | | | | |

Possible rule:

_____

_____

The Gilman family will have spent_____.

**3.** Hettie is stacking paper cups. Each stack of 15 cups is 6 inches high. What is the total height of 10 stacks of cups?

| Number of Stacks | 1 | 2 | 3 | 10 |
|---|---|---|---|---|
| Height (in.) | 6 | 12 | 18 | |

Possible rule:

_____

_____

The total height of 10 stacks is_____.

# Problem-Solving Strategy

## FIND A PATTERN

**Write a pattern and solve.**

1. The Teen Shop stores sweaters in boxes. There are 2 sweaters in the first box, 4 sweaters in the second box, 6 sweaters in the third box, and 8 sweaters in the fourth box. If this pattern continues, what is the total number of sweaters in 6 boxes?

   _____

2. A city bus stops at the shopping mall at 10:15 A.M., 11:45 A.M., 1:15 P.M., and 2:45 P.M. If this pattern continues, at what time will a city bus make a sixth stop at the mall?

   _____

3. Doug saved $1 the first week, $2 the second week, $4 the third week, and $8 the fourth week. If this pattern continues, how much will he save the sixth week?

   _____

## MIXED APPLICATIONS

**Choose a strategy and solve.**

| STRATEGIES |
| --- |
| • Write a Number Sentence • Work Backward Guess and Check • Find a Pattern |

4. Ryan typed 36 words per minute on his first typing test, 41 on his second test, 46 on his third test, and 51 on his fourth test. If this pattern continues, how may words per minute will he type on this fifth test?

   _____

5. Chico worked in the garden 3 times as long as Paul. Paul worked in the garden 2 hours less than Terry. Terry worked in the garden for 4 hours. How many hours did Chico work in the garden?

   _____

## WRITER'S CORNER

6. Explain the strategy you used to solve Exercise 5.

   _____

   _____

Name _____  Date _____

# Exploring Adding and Subtracting Decimals

**Find the sum and the difference for each pair of models.**

**1.**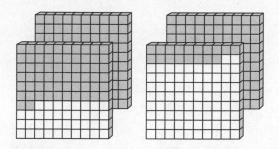

**2.**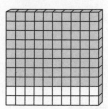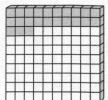

_____        _____

**Show each problem on the place-value chart. Solve.**

**3.** $4.6 + 3.84 + 15.07 = n.$

| Tens | Ones | Tenths | Hundredths |
|------|------|--------|------------|
|      | .    |        |            |
|      | .    |        |            |
|      | .    |        |            |
|      | .    |        |            |

**4.** $36.8 + 4.06 + 14.75 = n.$

| Tens | Ones | Tenths | Hundredths |
|------|------|--------|------------|
|      | .    |        |            |
|      | .    |        |            |
|      | .    |        |            |
|      | .    |        |            |

**5.** $9.1 - 3.7 = n.$

| Ones | Tenths |
|------|--------|
| .    |        |
| .    |        |
| .    |        |

**6.** $4.2 - 1.8 = n.$

| Ones | Tenths |
|------|--------|
| .    |        |
| .    |        |
| .    |        |

**7.** $18.62 - 12.8 = n.$

| Tens | Ones | Tenths | Hundredths |
|------|------|--------|------------|
|      | .    |        |            |
|      | .    |        |            |
|      | .    |        |            |

## MIXED REVIEW

**Circle the number in which the digit 6 has the greatest value.**

**8.** 80.632   6.825   0.068

**9.** 0.063   0.306   0.603

**Circle the number in which the digit 5 has the least value.**

**10.** 50.034   03.504   40.035

**11.** 0.385   0.258   0.582

**29**

# Adding Decimals

**Find the sum.**

| | | | | | | | | | |
|---|---|---|---|---|---|---|---|---|---|
| **1.** | 0.74<br>+ 0.08 | **2.** | 19.6<br>+ 4.7 | **3.** | 4.56<br>+ 0.96 | **4.** | 0.75<br>+ 8.57 | **5.** | 42.8<br>+ 9.7 |

| | | | | | | | | | |
|---|---|---|---|---|---|---|---|---|---|
| **6.** | 4.32<br>+ 2.49 | **7.** | 42.08<br>+ 16.43 | **8.** | 23.82<br>+ 18.56 | **9.** | 2.95<br>14.86<br>+ 9.09 | **10.** | 7.68<br>9.50<br>+ 8.94 |

**11.** $0.42 + 1.87 + 9 = n =$ _____ **12.** $2.67 + 5 + 0.38 = n =$ _____

**13.** $7.6 + 4.8 + 12 = n =$ _____ **14.** $18.09 + 32.45 + 6 = n =$ _____

## MIXED APPLICATIONS

**15.** A butcher shop receives a shipment of 57.3 kilograms of beef and 42.75 kilograms of chicken. What is the total weight of the shipment?

_____

**16.** At one store, a package of sliced turkey sells for $4.68. The store also offers 2 packages for $9.04. Which is the better buy?

_____

## LOGICAL REASONING

For Exercises 17–19, look at each mixed number and the decimal numbers to its right. Cross out any decimal number that is not equivalent to the given mixed number. (HINT: Rewrite the given mixed number as a decimal fraction. Example: $1\frac{1}{5} = 1\frac{2}{10} = 1.2 = 1.20$.)

**17.** $7\frac{1}{2}$    7.05    7.5    7.50    7.55

**18.** $9\frac{2}{5}$    90.4    9.4    9.04    9.2

**19.** $6\frac{3}{50}$    6.3    6.06    6.6    60.6

**30**

# Adding Tenths and Hundredths

**Estimate the sum by rounding each addend to the nearest whole number.**

**1.** $6.5 + 3.4 \approx$ _____

**2.** $45.4 + 7.6 \approx$ _____

**3.** $25.62 + 10.74 \approx$ _____

**4.** $254.56 + 45.03 \approx$ _____

**Find the sum.**

**5.**
$$\begin{array}{r} 0.98 \\ + 0.66 \\ \hline \end{array}$$

**6.**
$$\begin{array}{r} 4.18 \\ + 0.57 \\ \hline \end{array}$$

**7.**
$$\begin{array}{r} 6.15 \\ + 3.49 \\ \hline \end{array}$$

**8.**
$$\begin{array}{r} 7.35 \\ + 5.78 \\ \hline \end{array}$$

**9.**
$$\begin{array}{r} 23.56 \\ + 12.08 \\ \hline \end{array}$$

**10.**
$$\begin{array}{r} 43.36 \\ + 9.93 \\ \hline \end{array}$$

**11.**
$$\begin{array}{r} 250.61 \\ + 5.25 \\ \hline \end{array}$$

**12.**
$$\begin{array}{r} 200.34 \\ + 152.67 \\ \hline \end{array}$$

**13.** $43.25 + 56.93 = n =$ _____

**14.** $0.63 + 0.43 + 1.64 = n =$ _____

## MIXED APPLICATIONS

**15.** Heather went to the movies. She paid $3.75 for a ticket, $2.75 for popcorn, and $1.35 for juice. How much did she spend?

_____

**16.** A plate lunch costs $1.35. Bought separately, the items cost: sandwich, $0.95; milk, $0.35; and fruit, $0.20. Which is the less expensive way to buy the items?

_____

**17.** One model of tennis racket cost $83.75. This month the price increased by $15.43. What is the new price?

_____

**18.** The smallest dog on record is a Chihuahua that measured 9.84 inches from head to tail. Write this length in word form.

_____

## LOGICAL REASONING

**19.** If the value of 6 coins is $0.56, what are the coins?

_____

# Subtracting Decimals

**Find the difference.**

1.  7.8
    − 2.5

2.  5.63
    − 2.32

3.  5.46
    − 3.08

4.  9.40
    − 5.76

5.  8.36
    − 2.97

6.  25.00
    − 8.93

7.  42.06
    − 3.95

8.  72.45
    − 34.68

9.  5.49
    − 3.58

10.  16.09
    − 7.58

11. $8.6 - 4.74 = n =$ _____

12. $9.3 - 2.8 = n =$ _____

13. $9 - 3.16 = n =$ _____

14. $35 - 12.91 = n =$ _____

## MIXED APPLICATIONS

**Use the table to answer Exercises 15–18.**

15. How many seconds longer did it take Tom to run 200 meters than 100 meters?

    _____

16. What is Bianca's total running time for the two races?

    _____

| Junior Olympics Running Times (sec) | | |
|---|---|---|
| | 100 meters | 200 meters |
| Bianca | 21.52 | 42.3 |
| Tom | 20.85 | 43.8 |
| Suki | 22.84 | 44.6 |
| Joshua | 23.4 | 46 |
| Derrick | 24 | 45.87 |

17. In the 200-meter race, how many seconds faster is Suki's time than Joshua's?

    _____

18. What is Derrick's combined time for both races?

    _____

## WRITER'S CORNER

19. Write an addition and a subtraction word problem using the decimals 8.2 and 2.65.

    _____

    _____

# Subtracting Tenths and Hundredths

**Estimate the difference by rounding to the nearest whole number.**

1. $5.9 - 3.4 \approx$ _____

2. $5.0 - 0.7 \approx$ _____

3. $12.4 - 7.6 \approx$ _____

4. $23.42 - 12.52 \approx$ _____

**Find the difference.**

5.
$$\begin{array}{r} 4.69 \\ -\ 4.05 \\ \hline \end{array}$$

6.
$$\begin{array}{r} 48.06 \\ -\ 33.47 \\ \hline \end{array}$$

7.
$$\begin{array}{r} \$73.29 \\ -\ 8.72 \\ \hline \end{array}$$

8.
$$\begin{array}{r} 30.07 \\ -\ 30.04 \\ \hline \end{array}$$

9.
$$\begin{array}{r} \$125.73 \\ -\ 84.29 \\ \hline \end{array}$$

10.
$$\begin{array}{r} 0.43 \\ -\ 0.27 \\ \hline \end{array}$$

11.
$$\begin{array}{r} 836.59 \\ -\ 416.83 \\ \hline \end{array}$$

12.
$$\begin{array}{r} 500.02 \\ -\ 489.41 \\ \hline \end{array}$$

## MIXED APPLICATIONS

13. Kelsey is looking at two swimsuits. One swimsuit costs $30.45. A second swimsuit costs $17.90. How much more does the first suit cost?

_____

14. A diver won 36.32 points on his first dive, 23.95 points on his second dive, and 54.8 points on his third dive. What was the diver's score at the end of the third round?

_____

## VISUAL THINKING

**Write the amount of the decimal square that is shaded in decimal form.**

15.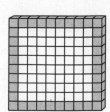

16.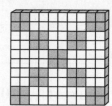

_____          _____

# Exploring Equivalent Decimals

**Write two equivalent decimals for each decimal.**

**1.** 0.8 _____

**2.** 1.30 _____

**3.** 3.0 _____

**4.** 6.400 _____

**Use equivalent decimals to rewrite one of the numbers in each problem so both numbers have the same number of decimal places.**

**5.** $1.2 + 4.56 = n$

**6.** $6.45 - 2 = n$

**7.** $8.7 - 0.02 = n$

**8.** $3.2 + 4.26 = n$

**Rewrite each problem as necessary. Then solve.**

**9.** $0.43 + 0.2 = n$

**10.** $0.8 + 0.52 = n$

**11.** $1.42 + 0.5 = n$

**12.** $4 + 23.17 = n$

**13.** $8.1 - 5.73 = n$

**14.** $3.86 - 0.8 = n$

---

## MIXED REVIEW

**Write the value of each number in expanded form.**

**15.** 304,218 _____

**16.** 34,556,000 _____

**Estimate to the nearest 1,000. Use the ≈ symbol.**

| **17.** | 406 | **18.** | 264,225 | **19.** | 7,230 | **20.** | 35,643 |
|---|---|---|---|---|---|---|---|
| | + 552 | | − 36,004 | | + 993 | | − 11,535 |

Name _____ Date _____

# Using Mental Math with Multiples of Ten

**Use mental math to find each product.**

| 1. | 80 | 2. | 900 | 3. | 2,000 | 4. | 6,000 | 5. | 5,000 |
|----|----|----|----|----|----|----|----|----|----|
| | × 7 | | × 4 | | × 8 | | × 9 | | × 8 |

**Complete each number sentence by using mental math.**

6. $3 \times 400 =$ _____       7. _____ $\times 40 = 160$     **8.** $70 \times 6 =$ _____

9. $500 \times 6 =$ _____    **10.** $9 \times$ _____ $= 5,400$   **11.** _____ $\times 70 = 560$

**Multiply each number by 10, 100, and 1,000.**

12. 6 _____, _____, _____       13. 3 _____, _____, _____

14. 7 _____, _____, _____       15. 5 _____, _____, _____

## MIXED APPLICATIONS

**Use the table to solve Exercises 16–17.**

16. How many more miles in all
    did Bernard drive than George?

    _____

17. On which day was the greatest
    number of miles driven?

    _____

| Number of Miles Driven | | | |
|----|----|----|----|
| **Driver** | **Monday** | **Tuesday** | **Wednesday** |
| George | 20 | 25 | 49 |
| Caridad | 30 | 50 | 70 |
| Bernard | 26 | 42 | 35 |

## LOGICAL REASONING

18. When completed, the magic square will show
    the digits 1–9. Each row, each column, and
    each diagonal will have a sum of 15. Fill in
    the missing digits to complete the square.

| | | 6 |
|----|----|----|
| | 5 | |
| 3 | | |

**35**

Unit 4
Core Skills Math, Grade 5

# Multiplying: Practice

**Find the product.**

| | | | | |
|---|---|---|---|---|
| 1. 345 $\times$ 12 | 2. 342 $\times$ 68 | 3. 164 $\times$ 53 | 4. 304 $\times$ 82 | 5. 657 $\times$ 89 |

6. $89 \times 508 =$ _____

7. $62 \times 258 =$ _____

8. $56 \times 613 =$ _____

## MIXED APPLICATIONS

9. There are 123 dancers in the ballet. Each dancer has 12 costumes. How many costumes are there?

_____

10. In one ballet, there are 14 adult male dancers, 14 adult female dancers, and 10 young dancers. How many dancers are there?

_____

## EVERYDAY MATH CONNECTION

**Al is looking for a part-time job. The table lists the jobs he has applied for and their weekly salary.**

11. Complete the Yearly Salary column. Remember, 1 year = 52 weeks.

12. Which job pays the highest salary?

_____

13. How much more money would Al earn per year as a delivery person than as a dishwasher?

_____

| Part-time Jobs — Salaries | | |
|---|---|---|
| Job | Salary | |
| | Weekly | Yearly |
| Typist | $85 | |
| Dishwasher | $90 | |
| Cashier | $115 | |
| Stock clerk | $72 | |
| Delivery person | $120 | |

14. What are some questions Al might want to ask before accepting a job offer?

_____

_____

# Using Multiplication

**Use any method to estimate the product. Then solve.**

| 1. 108 | 2. 463 | 3. 2,786 | 4. 8,157 | 5. 20,016 |
|---|---|---|---|---|
| $\times\ 87$ | $\times\ 34$ | $\times\ 43$ | $\times\ 92$ | $\times\ 45$ |

**6.** $40 \times 768 = $ _____

**7.** $24 \times 5,063 = $ _____

**8.** $36 \times 895 = $ _____

**9.** $74 \times 10,572 = $ _____

**Barbara placed an order with a wholesale bulb company for her garden center. Complete the table.**

| Barbara's Bulb Order | | | |
|---|---|---|---|
| Type of Bulb | Number of Cartons | Bulbs per Carton | Total Number of Bulbs |
| **10.** Crocus | 42 | 250 | |
| **11.** Tulip | 865 | 75 | |
| **12.** Daffodil | 460 | 50 | |

## MIXED APPLICATIONS

**13.** Barbara plants 15 tulip bulbs in each of 150 clay pots. How many bulbs is this?

_____

**14.** Mrs. Daley buys 8 amaryllis bulbs. Each bulb costs $8.79. If she gives the clerk $80, how much change should she receive?

_____

## MIXED REVIEW

**Find the product.**

| 15. $0.84 | 16. $1.56 | 17. $3.09 | 18. 156 | 19. 825 |
|---|---|---|---|---|
| $\times\ 6$ | $\times\ 9$ | $\times\ 4$ | $\times\ 97$ | $\times\ 88$ |

**37**

# Multiplying by 2-Digit Numbers

**Find the product.**

| 1. | 61 | 2. | 23 | 3. | 92 | 4. | 77 | 5. | 317 |
|---|---|---|---|---|---|---|---|---|---|
| | × 24 | | × 12 | | × 82 | | × 27 | | × 34 |

| 6. | 302 | 7. | 432 | 8. | 501 | 9. | 578 | 10. | 329 |
|---|---|---|---|---|---|---|---|---|---|
| | × 41 | | × 68 | | × 65 | | × 57 | | × 84 |

11. 29 × 23 = _____     12. 459 × 38 = _____

13. 485 × 42 = _____     14. 958 × 67 = _____

## MIXED APPLICATIONS

15. There are 2 teams of 15 wrestlers. If each wrestler must have 2 pairs of shoes, how many pairs of shoes are needed?

_____

16. The buses that take the teams to the matches each hold 40 players. If there are 15 buses going to a match, what is the greatest number of players that can go by bus?

_____

## HEALTH CONNECTION

**One gram (g) of fat contains 9 calories. Find the number of calories from fat in each serving of food.**

| | Food | Fat Content (in grams) | Fat Calories |
|---|---|---|---|
| 17. | 1 egg | 6 | |
| 18. | 1 tbsp. mayonnaise | 11 | |
| 19. | 1/2 cup vanilla ice cream | 7 | |
| 20. | 1 oz cheddar cheese | 9 | |
| 21. | 1 cup whole milk | 8 | |
| 22. | 2 oz cooked crab meat | 1 | |

Unit 4
Core Skills Math, Grade 5

# Multiplying by 3-Digit Numbers

**Use any method to estimate the product. Use ≈ in the answer.**

| 1. | 234 | 2. | 732 | 3. | 706 | 4. | 749 | 5. | 559 |
|----|-----|----|-----|----|-----|----|-----|----|-----|
|    | × 323 |  | × 487 |  | × 537 |  | × 594 |  | × 438 |

**Find the product.**

| 6. | 584 | 7. | 563 | 8. | 265 | 9. | 508 | 10. | 379 |
|----|-----|----|-----|----|-----|----|-----|-----|-----|
|    | × 371 |  | × 384 |  | × 846 |  | × 730 |  | × 218 |

| 11. | 4,597 | 12. | 3,084 | 13. | 9,624 | 14. | 7,246 | 15. | 4,800 |
|-----|-------|-----|-------|-----|-------|-----|-------|-----|-------|
|     | × 471 |   | × 532 |   | × 248 |   | × 342 |   | × 300 |

## MIXED APPLICATIONS

**Solve.**

**16.** There are 20 houses on Essex Street. Every third house has a streetlight in front of it. How many houses do not have a streetlight?

_____

**17.** For the past 36 years, Charlie has eaten 3 meals a day. How many meals has he eaten in that time? Use 1 year = 365 days.

_____

**18.** Use a calculator to find the number that when multiplied by itself has a product of 9,604.

_____

**19.** If Darren had $15.00 more, he could buy a radio that costs $84.95. How much money does Darren have?

_____

## NUMBER SENSE

**For Exercises 20–21, use each of the digits 0–9 once.**

**20.** Write the two 5-digit numbers that have the greatest difference. _____

**21.** Write the two 5-digit numbers that have the least difference. _____

# Multiplying by 2- and 3-Digit Numbers

**Estimate the product. If your estimate is greater than 200,000, use a calculator to find the exact answer.**

1.  903
    × 46

2.  4,899
    × 607

3.  612
    × 24

4.  7,842
    × 84

5. 7,503 × 304 _____     6. 792 × 85 _____     7. 4,245 × 57 _____

**Find the product.**

8.   68
     × 76

9.   74
     × 93

10.  2,987
     × 33

11.  1,344
     × 803

12.  46,099
     × 35

13.  235
     × 476

14.  2,356
     × 758

15. 156,472
     × 56

16.  10,200
     × 503

17.  12,030
     × 607

18.  536
     × 478

19.  5,721
     × 587

20.  7,124
     × 63

21.  56,812
     × 467

22.  123,976
     × 783

## MIXED APPLICATIONS

23. Mr. Schmidt ordered 48 typewriters for his office. Each typewriter cost $195. About how much did the typewriters cost?

_____

24. There are 264 oranges in a large crate. How many oranges are in 25 crates?

_____

## NUMBER SENSE

**Use mental math and estimation to compare the numbers. Write <, >, or =.**

25. 45 × 10 ◯ 5.8 × 100          26. $1.75 \times 10^3$ ◯ 175 × 10

27. $2^4$ ◯ $5^2$

# Multiplying with Regrouping

**Find the product. A place-value chart can help you with regrouping and placing zeros in the partial products.**

**1.**

| Th | H | T | O |
|----|---|---|---|
|    |   | 2 |   |
|    |   | 5 |   |
|    |   | 4 | 7 |
| ×  |   | 3 | 8 |
|    | 3 | 7 | 6 |
| + 1 | 4 | 1 | 0 |
|    |   |   |   |

**2.**

| Th | H | T | O |
|----|---|---|---|
|    | 3 | 5 | 6 |
| ×  |   | 2 | 4 |

**3.**

| Th | H | T | O |
|----|---|---|---|
|    | 1 | 4 | 6 |
| ×  |   | 5 | 2 |

**4.**

| Th | H | T | O |
|----|---|---|---|
|    | 4 | 7 | 6 |
| ×  |   | 3 | 8 |

**5.**   57
      × 38

**6.**   245
      × 4

**7.**   436
      × 29

**8.**   238
      × 49

**9.**   537
      × 8

**10.**   86
       × 64

**11.**   209
       × 53

**12.**   784
       × 9

**13.**   98
       × 75

**14.**   514
       × 46

**15.**   304
       × 95

**16.**   273
       × 28

**17.**   511
       × 50

**18.**   128
       × 264

**19.**   539
       × 645

# Multiplication Practice

**Find the product.**

| **1.** 231 | **2.** 412 | **3.** 112 | **4.** 332 | **5.** 212 |
|---|---|---|---|---|
| × 3 | × 2 | × 4 | × 3 | × 4 |

| **6.** 769 | **7.** 825 | **8.** 892 | **9.** 483 | **10.** 536 |
|---|---|---|---|---|
| × 8 | × 6 | × 8 | × 9 | × 7 |

| **11.** 849 | **12.** 675 | **13.** 892 | **14.** 684 | **15.** 324 |
|---|---|---|---|---|
| × 8 | × 9 | × 5 | × 7 | × 8 |

**Find the product. Use mental math if possible.**

| **16.** 18 | **17.** 56 | **18.** 49 | **19.** 37 | **20.** 24 |
|---|---|---|---|---|
| × 70 | × 20 | × 30 | × 50 | × 10 |

**Find the product. Add zeros to the partial products as necessary.**

| **21.** 53 | **22.** 46 | **23.** 90 | **24.** 38 | **25.** 28 |
|---|---|---|---|---|
| × 25 | × 47 | × 58 | × 57 | × 16 |

| **26.** 456 | **27.** 308 | **28.** 764 | **29.** 354 | **30.** 418 |
|---|---|---|---|---|
| × 13 | × 18 | × 46 | × 55 | × 23 |

**42**

# Polygons

Name each polygon by the number of sides it has. Then tell whether it is a *regular polygon* or *not a regular polygon*.

**1.**

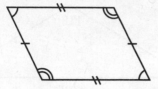

4 sides, 4 vertices, 4 angles means

it is a _____ .

The sides are not all congruent, so it is

_____ .

**2.**

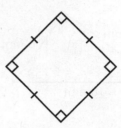

_____

_____

**3.**

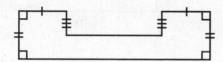

_____

_____

**4.**

_____

_____

**5.**

_____

_____

**6.**

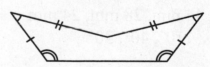

_____

_____

# Triangles

**Classify each triangle by side lengths and angle measures. Write *isosceles*, *scalene*, or *equilateral*. Then write *acute*, *obtuse*, or *right*.**

**1.**

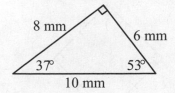

None of the side measures are equal.
So, it is _____.
There is a right angle, so it is
a _____ triangle.

**2.**

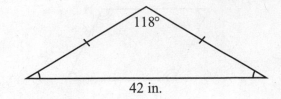

_____  _____

**3.**

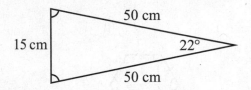

_____  _____

**4.**

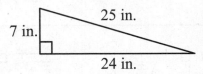

_____  _____

**A triangle has sides with the lengths and angle measures given. Classify each triangle. Write *isosceles*, *scalene*, or *equilateral*. Then write *acute*, *obtuse*, or *right*. Draw a sketch if it is helpful.**

**5.** sides: 44 mm, 28 mm, 24 mm
angles: 110°, 40°, 30°

_____  _____

**6.** sides: 23 mm, 20 mm, 13 mm
angles: 62°, 72°, 46°

_____  _____

---

## MIXED APPLICATIONS

**7.** Mary says her garden is shaped like an acute right triangle. Is this possible? Explain.

_____

**8.** Karen says every equilateral triangle is also an acute triangle. Is this true? Explain.

_____

Name _____ Date _____

# Exploring Other Polygons

**Name the polygon represented by each traffic sign.**

1.

2.

3.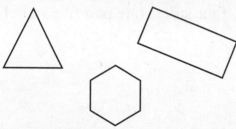

4.

_____    _____    _____    _____

5. Circle the polygons that appear regular.

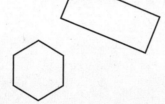 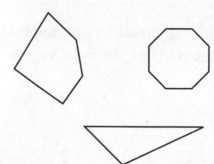

**Write *true* or *false*.**

6. A regular octagon has eight sides of equal length. _____

7. A pentagon has six sides and six angles. _____

8. A regular quadrilateral has four sides of equal length. _____

9. A triangle has four angles. _____

10. A figure with six sides is called a hexagon. _____

11. A circle is a special type of polygon. _____

## ENGLISH CONNECTION

12. Use a dictionary to find the meaning of the prefixes: *quad-*, *tri-*, *penta-*, *hexa-*, and *octa-*. Write the definitions. Then make a list of words that begin with each prefix.

_____

_____

_____

**45**

# Exploring Quadrilaterals

**For Exercises 1–4, draw and give the most specific name for each quadrilateral described.**

1. opposite sides are parallel and equal; no right angles

2. four sides of equal length; four right angles

_____

3. four sides of equal length; opposite sides are parallel; no right angles

4. four sides; one pair of parallel sides

_____

_____

5. Manny cut out a figure and labeled it a rectangle. His friend called it a square. Could they both be correct? Explain?

_____

6. Jennifer drew a square on the sidewalk. One side measures 35 inches. If she walks halfway around the square, how many inches will she walk? If she walks all the way around, how many inches will she walk?

_____

## VISUAL THINKING

7. How many different squares with whole number side measures can you draw on a 5-by-5 square? (HINT: Use grid paper, draw diagrams, and make a table.)

| Length of side | 1 | 2 | 3 | 4 | 5 |
|---|---|---|---|---|---|
| Number of squares | | | | | |

Total number of squares _____

Name _____  Date _____

# Quadrilaterals and Other Polygons

**Classify each figure in one way. Write:** *rectangle, trapezoid, square, rhombus,* **or**
*parallelogram.* **Use a name only once.**

1. quadrilateral with opposite sides parallel _____

2. parallelogram with four right angles _____

3. rectangle with four congruent sides _____

4. exactly one pair opposite sides parallel _____

5. opposite sides parallel and congruent _____

**Classify each figure as regular or irregular.**

6.    7.    8.    9.

_____  _____  _____  _____

---

## MIXED APPLICATIONS

10. Look around your classroom. Name at least three examples of polygons in the room.

_____

_____

11. What is the ratio of squares to triangles in the pattern shown?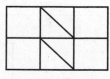

_____

## LOGICAL REASONING

12. Can a square also be a rhombus? Explain.

_____

_____

13. Is a triangle a polygon and a quadrilateral? Explain.

_____

_____

# Quadrilaterals

**Classify the quadrilateral in as many ways as possible.**
**Write *quadrilateral*, *parallelogram*, *rectangle*, *rhombus*, *square*, or *trapezoid*.**

**1.**

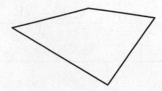

It has 4 sides, so it is a

_____. None of the

sides are parallel, so there is

_____.

**2.**

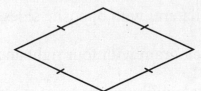

_____

**3.**

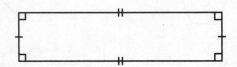

_____

**4.**

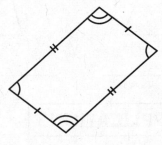

_____

**5.**

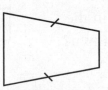

_____

**6.**

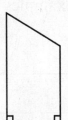

_____

---

**MIXED APPLICATIONS**

**7.** Kevin claims he can draw a trapezoid with three right angles. Is this possible? Explain.

_____

**8.** "If a figure is a square, then it is a regular quadrilateral." Is this true or false? Explain.

_____

# Exploring Relationships Among Quadrilaterals

**Use the figure for Exercises 1–3.**

1. Name a rectangle on the figure.

   _____

2. Name a parallelogram that is not a rectangle.

   _____

3. Name three trapezoids.

   _____

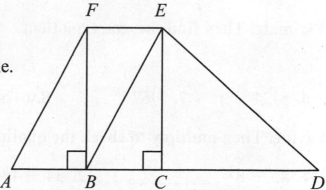

**Identify each figure. Write all that apply:** *quadrilateral, trapezoid, parallelogram, rectangle, rhombus,* **or** *square.*

4. A parallelogram with congruent sides and no right angles is a

   _____.

5. A quadrilateral with exactly one pair of parallel sides is a

   _____.

**Read each statement. Write** *always, sometimes,* **or** *never.*

6. A rhombus is a square.

   _____

7. A square is a rhombus.

   _____

8. A trapezoid is a parallelogram.

   _____

9. A polygon is a quadrilateral.

   _____

## VISUAL THINKING

Draw one line segment inside each figure to form the two figures described.

10.

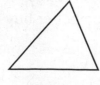

a triangle and
a trapezoid

11.

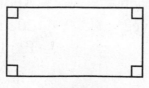

two trapezoids

12.

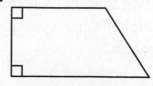

a trapezoid and
a rectangle

# Dividing 2-Digit Numbers

**Use multiplication facts to estimate each quotient.**

1. $5\overline{)37}$     2. $2\overline{)23}$     3. $5\overline{)62}$     4. $7\overline{)69}$     5. $9\overline{)91}$

**Estimate. Then find the exact quotient.**

6. $5\overline{)24}$     7. $7\overline{)67}$     8. $6\overline{)74}$     9. $9\overline{)93}$     10. $9\overline{)103}$

**Divide. Then multiply to check the quotient.**

11. $45 \div 8 =$ _____     12. $34 \div 4 =$ _____     13. $54 \div 5 =$ _____

14. $82 \div 9 =$ _____     15. $86 \div 8 =$ _____     16. $47 \div 8 =$ _____

17. $13 \div 9 =$ _____     18. $96 \div 8 =$ _____

## MIXED APPLICATIONS

19. One section of a stadium has 122 seats and 11 rows. There are about the same number of seats in each row.  About how many seats are there per row?

_____

20. The 22 students in Marie's class sold 132 tickets to the play. Each student sold the same number of tickets. How many tickets did each student sell?

_____

## EVERYDAY MATH CONNECTION

**Many consumers compare prices as they shop. Sometimes you need to divide to compare prices.  In these cases, estimating a quotient is helpful. Use estimation for Exercises 21–22.**

21. Carl needs 3 notepads. Block brand notepads cost 95¢ for a package of 3. Welsh brand notepads cost 25¢ each. Which notepads are less expensive? Explain.

_____

_____

22. Daisy needs 3 oranges. At one fruit stand they cost 98¢ for a half dozen. Another fruit stand has oranges for 20¢ each. Which is the better buy? Explain.

_____

_____

# Dividing 3-Digit Numbers

**Estimate each quotient. If the estimate is greater than 50, find the exact quotient.**

**1.** $135 \div 3 \approx$ _____

**2.** $328 \div 4 \approx$ _____

**3.** $539 \div 6 \approx$ _____

**Find the exact quotient.**

**4.** $7\overline{)542}$

**5.** $8\overline{)638}$

**6.** $3\overline{)461}$

**7.** $7\overline{)874}$

**8.** $5\overline{)783}$

**9.** $156 \div 7 = n$ _____

**10.** $189 \div 8 = n$ _____

**11.** $430 \div 4 = n$ _____

**12.** $593 \div 7 = n$ _____

## MIXED APPLICATIONS

**13.** For a crafts project, 9 students divide 537 toothpicks evenly among them. How many toothpicks does each student get? How many are left over?

**14.** The students at North School went on a field trip with 14 teachers. Each teacher took 13 students. How many people went on the trip?

_____

_____

## NUMBER SENSE

**15.** Demonstrate that division is repeated subtraction of the same quantity. Write a division problem that has a two-digit dividend and a one-digit divisor that will not divide evenly.

- Find the answer using division.

- Find it using repeated subtraction and tell what the quotient and the remainder represent.

 ____ ____ ÷ ____ = _____

# Short Division

Use short division to find each quotient. Do the steps mentally instead of writing them down.

1. $3\overline{)49}$       2. $6\overline{)74}$       3. $4\overline{)94}$       4. $8\overline{)429}$       5. $6\overline{)290}$

6. $7\overline{)873}$      7. $4\overline{)341}$      8. $8\overline{)593}$      9. $9\overline{)692}$      10. $6\overline{)942}$

11. $7\overline{)452}$     12. $9\overline{)568}$     13. $5\overline{)665}$     14. $4\overline{)532}$     15. $8\overline{)690}$

16. $241 \div 5 =$ _____       17. $750 \div 4 =$ _____       18. $573 \div 7 =$ _____

19. $959 \div 9 =$ _____       20. $948 \div 7 =$ _____       21. $485 \div 3 =$ _____

## MIXED APPLICATIONS

22. Miki drove 397 miles in 8 hours. About how many miles did she drive each hour?

_____

23. At the boat show, 11 boats were presented each hour. On Tuesday the show lasted 14 hours. How many boats were shown on Tuesday?

_____

24. Mary has 503 stamps. She plans to put an equal number of stamps in each of 7 stamp albums. Estimate the number of stamps Mary will put in each album.

_____

25. Joe has 160 books to put on 5 shelves. He puts the same number of books on each shelf. How many books are on each shelf? How many will not fit?

_____

## LANGUAGE ARTS CONNECTION

26. Use the numbers 7 and 809 to write two word problems that can be solved using short division.

_____

_____

# Zeros in the Quotient

**Find the quotient.**

1. 4)360     2. 8)523     3. 4)805     4. 9)633     5. 3)6,720

6. 5)250     7. 7)420     8. 6)480     9. 4)522     10. 6)623

11. 2)616     12. 9)923     13. 6)605     14. 3)205     15. 4)812

## MIXED APPLICATIONS

16. Sonya went on a river cruise. There were 132 people waiting for 4 boats. If the same number of people got on each boat, how many were on each boat?

   _____

17. At a different pier, 65 people were waiting to board boats. The boats at this pier can hold 30 people. How many boats are needed for the 65 people?

   _____

18. A clerk spilled 1,830 paper clips on the floor. Each of 6 salespeople picked up the same number of paper clips. How many paper clips did each salesperson pick up?

   _____

19. For the problem 704 ÷ 7, Martell got the quotient 16. Is this a reasonable answer? Explain.

   _____

## MIXED REVIEW

**Find the quotient.**

20. 90 ÷ 6 = _____     21. 147 ÷ 7 = _____

22. 321 ÷ 6 = _____     23. 596 ÷ 9 = _____

**Write each number as the product of a whole number and a power of ten.**

24. 9,000 _____     25. 500 _____

26. 40,000 _____     27. 600,000 _____

**53**

# Division Patterns

**Find the quotient.**

**1.** $60 \div 30 =$ _____     **2.** $80 \div 20 =$ _____     **3.** $360 \div 40 =$ _____

**4.** $420 \div 70 =$ _____     **5.** $5{,}600 \div 80 =$ _____     **6.** $45{,}000 \div 90 =$ _____

**7.** $30\overline{)60}$          **8.** $10\overline{)70}$          **9.** $40\overline{)80}$          **10.** $60\overline{)60}$

**11.** $30\overline{)900}$          **12.** $60\overline{)120}$          **13.** $50\overline{)250}$          **14.** $70\overline{)280}$

**15.** $20\overline{)800}$          **16.** $40\overline{)4{,}000}$          **17.** $30\overline{)9{,}000}$          **18.** $90\overline{)8{,}100}$

**19.** $10\overline{)1{,}000}$          **20.** $30\overline{)2{,}100}$          **21.** $20\overline{)8{,}000}$          **22.** $30\overline{)60{,}000}$

## MIXED APPLICATIONS

**23.** For a science project, Ms. Ramon handed out 300 bean seedlings for the class to plant. If each of the 30 students got the same number of seedlings, how many seedlings did each student receive?

_____

**24.** Each day the students gave each of the 300 seedlings exactly 40 drops of water. How many drops of water did the students use every day to water the plants?

_____

## SCIENCE CONNECTION

**25.** Using division patterns, write a word problem about a class science project. Solve.

_____

_____

_____

54

# Division with 2-Digit Divisors

**Use the quick picture to divide. The square, lines, and circles represent the dividend.**

**1.** $132 \div 12 =$ _____

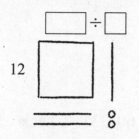

**2.** $168 \div 14 =$ _____

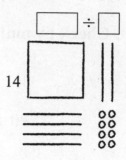

**Divide. Use base-ten blocks.**

**3.** $195 \div 13 =$ _____      **4.** $143 \div 11 =$ _____      **5.** $165 \div 15 =$ _____

**Divide. Draw a quick picture.**

**6.** $192 \div 16 =$ _____          **7.** $169 \div 13 =$ _____

---

## MIXED APPLICATIONS

**8.** There are 182 seats in a theater. The seats are evenly divided into 13 rows. How many seats are in each row?

_____

**9.** There are 156 students at summer camp. The camp has 13 cabins. An equal number of students sleep in each cabin. How many students sleep in each cabin?

_____

# Dividing by Tens with Remainders

Draw a ☐ where the first digit in the quotient should be placed.

**1.** $60\overline{)365}$     **2.** $40\overline{)250}$     **3.** $70\overline{)295}$     **4.** $90\overline{)189}$     **5.** $50\overline{)475}$

**Estimate the quotient. Check by multiplying.**

**6.** $30\overline{)68}$   Check     **7.** $20\overline{)88}$   Check     **8.** $60\overline{)331}$   Check

**9.** $50\overline{)268}$   Check     **10.** $40\overline{)295}$   Check     **11.** $80\overline{)500}$   Check

## MIXED APPLICATIONS

**12.** A radio station gave sun visors to 270 people on Fun Day. There were 30 visors in each carton. How many cartons of visors did the station give away?

_____

**13.** The station also sold 140 tickets for a raffle on Fun Day. Each raffle ticket cost 50 cents. How much did the station collect from raffle ticket sales?

_____

## SOCIAL STUDIES CONNECTION

**14.** The cost of mailing a first-class letter has increased many times since the mid-1800s. The costs below show the increase in the price of a sheet of 20 first-class stamps since 1995. Find the cost of one stamp.

| 1995 | 1999 | 2001 | 2002 | 2006 | 2009 | 2012 |
|------|------|------|------|------|------|------|
| $6.40 | $6.60 | $6.80 | $7.40 | $7.80 | $8.80 | $9.00 |

_____ _____ _____ _____ _____ _____ _____

Name _____ Date _____

# Exploring Dividing with 2-Digit Divisors

**Find each quotient. Draw a quick picture or use place-value blocks to help you.**

1. $12\overline{)49}$      2. $24\overline{)98}$      3. $31\overline{)94}$      4. $20\overline{)67}$

5. $21\overline{)108}$      6. $42\overline{)169}$      7. $90\overline{)237}$      8. $85\overline{)425}$

9. $72\overline{)377}$      10. $63\overline{)260}$      11. $19\overline{)143}$      12. $47\overline{)255}$

13. $32\overline{)224}$      14. $52\overline{)321}$      15. $29\overline{)281}$      16. $38\overline{)230}$

---

## WRITER'S CORNER

17. Explain the steps for dividing 699 by 86. Write as if you were thinking aloud, so someone else could follow the steps and understand your solution.

_____

_____

_____

# More 2-Digit Divisors

**Find each quotient.**

1. 53)‾106‾

2. 44)‾243‾

3. 64)‾320‾

4. 32)‾224‾

5. 35)‾142‾

6. 23)‾115‾

7. 77)‾539‾

8. 93)‾651‾

9. 42)‾252‾

10. 85)‾686‾

11. 65)‾391‾

12. 29)‾116‾

13. 74)‾592‾

14. 21)‾126‾

15. 91)‾646‾

16. 82)‾332‾

## MIXED APPLICATIONS

17. A science museum has an average of 424 visitors each day. The museum is open every day. Over a two-week period, how many people visit the museum?

18. On Monday, 138 students will take the subway to the museum. Each subway car holds 36 people. What is the smallest number of subway cars the students can use?

## LOGICAL REASONING

19. Find six pairs of numbers that could be substituted for $n$ and $x$ in the sentence $n \div x = 50$.

$n =$ _____   $n =$ _____   $n =$ _____   $n =$ _____   $n =$ _____   $n =$ _____

$x =$ _____   $x =$ _____   $x =$ _____   $x =$ _____   $x =$ _____   $x =$ _____

# 2-Digit Quotients

Draw a ☐ where the first digit in the quotient should be placed.

1. $43\overline{)567}$    2. $29\overline{)304}$    3. $17\overline{)249}$    4. $63\overline{)495}$    5. $23\overline{)96}$

Estimate the quotient by using compatible numbers. Then use a calculator to find the quotient by using repeated subtraction.

6. Estimate _____    $43\overline{)97}$    7. Estimate _____    $67\overline{)250}$

8. Estimate _____    $32\overline{)135}$    9. Estimate _____    $83\overline{)175}$

Find the quotient.

10. $28\overline{)793}$    11. $36\overline{)582}$    12. $70\overline{)856}$    13. $42\overline{)652}$

## MIXED APPLICATIONS

The table shows the approximate weight of one cubic yard of three different garden products. Use the table for Exercises 14–16.

14. How many 50-lb bags of mulch can be filled using 1 cu yd of mulch?

_____

| Product | Weight (per cu yd) |
|---------|--------------------|
| topsoil | 2,200 lb |
| compost | 1,400 lb |
| mulch | 400 lb |

15. Dan bought 1 cu yd of one of the products and filled twenty-eight 50-lb bags. What product did he buy?

_____

16. Darla has 2 cubic yards of topsoil. She has 50-lb, 30-lb, and 10-lb bags. If she wants to bag the topsoil using only one size of bags with no soil left over, what size bags

can she use? _____

## WRITER'S CORNER

17. Explain how you decide where the first digit in a quotient should be placed.

_____

_____

**59**

# Dividing Money

**Find the quotient. You may use a calculator.**

1. $17)\overline{\$612}$    2. $34)\overline{\$204}$    3. $14)\overline{\$322}$    4. $39)\overline{\$468}$    5. $23)\overline{\$644}$

6. $13)\overline{\$377}$    7. $59)\overline{\$826}$    8. $33)\overline{\$297}$    9. $17)\overline{\$476}$    10. $21)\overline{\$483}$

## MIXED APPLICATIONS

11. In the first hour of a street fair, Ron's Snapshots made $460 in sales. At $20 per snapshot, how many snapshots were sold?

_____

12. If Ron's Snapshots continues to earn $460 per hour, how much money will the company earn during the 6-hour street fair?

_____

13. For another event, Ron paid 3 photographers $53 a shift to snap photos. Complete the table to show the number of shifts each photographer worked.

14. If each shift was 4 hours, what is the total number of hours the photographers worked?

_____

| Ron's Snapshot Company | | |
|---|---|---|
| **Photographer** | **Shifts Worked** | **Pay** |
| Hans | | $689 |
| Rena | | $477 |
| Marika | | $954 |

## EVERYDAY MATH CONNECTION

15. Find the price per pound for each item.

| Vinnie's Market – Weekly Specials | | | |
|---|---|---|---|
| **Turkey** | **Lean Ground Beef** | **Fresh Salmon** | **Chicken Tenders** |
| 11 lb   $22 | 15 lb   $60 | 9 lb   $72 | 12 lb   $36 |

_____   _____   _____   _____

# Dividing 2-Digit Numbers

**Estimate each quotient.**

**1.** $87 \div 32 \approx$ _____     **2.** $59 \div 25 \approx$ _____     **3.** $76 \div 38 \approx$ _____

**Divide. Use multiplication to check.**

**4.** $21\overline{)42}$          **5.** $35\overline{)65}$          **6.** $17\overline{)85}$          **7.** $23\overline{)72}$

**8.** $51\overline{)70}$          **9.** $33\overline{)98}$          **10.** $25\overline{)80}$          **11.** $41\overline{)95}$

**12.** $11\overline{)75}$          **13.** $50\overline{)79}$          **14.** $62\overline{)78}$          **15.** $10\overline{)93}$

**16.** $89 \div 30 =$ _____     **17.** $66 \div 13 =$ _____     **18.** $48 \div 20 =$ _____

**19.** $59 \div 19 =$ _____     **20.** $80 \div 17 =$ _____     **21.** $97 \div 44 =$ _____

## MIXED APPLICATIONS

**22.** Alana wants to buy some socks that cost $3 per pair. She has $11. How many pairs of socks can she buy? How much money will she have left?

**23.** Jim's van can hold 7 people plus a driver. If he wants to take 18 friends to the beach, how many trips will he need to make?

**24.** Mr. Youngbear buys T-shirts in boxes of 20 for $80 per box. He sells the T-shirts for $6 each. How much profit has he made after selling 93 T-shirts?

**25.** Maria made 12 hand-painted hairclips. If she sells them for 2 for $3.00, will she have enough money to buy a shirt that costs $18 after tax?

## SCIENCE CONNECTION

**26.** Many light bulbs manufactured today last up to 5 times as long as those made 30 years ago. If a new light bulb has an average life of 35,000 hours, what was the life, in hours, of the older bulbs?

# Quotients

**Circle the better estimate for the first digit in the quotient. Choose a. or b.**

1. $21\overline{)179}$           2. $57\overline{)286}$           3. $42\overline{)304}$           4. $18\overline{)170}$

  **a.** 8  **b.** 9        **a.** 4  **b.** 5        **a.** 7  **b.** 8        **a.** 9  **b.** 10

**Divide.**

5. $45\overline{)322}$           6. $24\overline{)89}$           7. $28\overline{)141}$           8. $62\overline{)376}$

9. $42\overline{)236}$           10. $34\overline{)226}$           11. $38\overline{)127}$           12. $69\overline{)272}$

## MIXED APPLICATIONS

13. The principal asked for volunteers to prepare booths for the fall fair. The principal wants no more than 6 students per group with 1 teacher per group to help. If 40 students volunteer, how many teachers will be needed?

_____

14. Each of the 40 students worked 2 hours after school on Tuesdays and Thursdays. Also, 18 of the students worked 3 hours on Saturdays. If the work took two weeks, what is the total number of hours that the students worked?

_____

## MIXED REVIEW

**Divide.**

15. $12\overline{)360}$     16. $11\overline{)7,934}$     17. $11\overline{)1,111}$     18. $38\overline{)3,921}$     19. $27\overline{)21,340}$

**Multiply by 10, 100, and 1,000. Write the products below the numbers.**

20. 8           21. 12           22. 39           23. 54           24. 70

# Dividing 3-Digit Numbers

**Find the quotient.**

1. 22)‾874  2. 35)‾852  3. 17)‾849  4. 27)‾570

5. 18)‾743  6. 34)‾283  7. 46)‾174  8. 65)‾325

9. 51)‾757  10. 57)‾567  11. 32)‾811  12. 48)‾993

## MIXED APPLICATIONS

13. Marianne has 120 spoons in her collection. She wants to buy display cases for them. One type of case can hold 42 spoons. How many of these cases would she need to hold all the spoons? How many more spoons would she need to fill the cases?

14. Roberto has 262 dimes in his coin collection. One week he collected 5 more dimes. The next week he collected 8 more dimes, and in the third week he collected 11 more dimes. If this pattern continues, how many dimes will Roberto have at the end of 5 weeks?

## NUMBER SENSE

15. The Johnson family puts $1 in their money jar for every $6 they spend on entertainment. After 6 months, they have spent $2,376 on entertainment. How much money should be in the money jar?

16. If they continue to save at this rate, how many more months will it take them to save $1,000?

# Dividing Larger Numbers

**Estimate. Then find the quotient.**

1. 16)3,945          2. 24)8,302          3. 66)6,000          4. 75)6,324

5. 39)1,631          6. 59)3,746          7. 81)5,450          8. 63)4,109

**Divide.**

9. 27)1,053          10. 33)3,069          11. 63)6,552          12. 78)6,084

13. 18)1,170          14. 41)2,214          15. 58)1,508          16. 39)1,794

## MIXED APPLICATIONS

17. If Rob drives 1,200 miles in 22 hours, is his average speed more than 55 miles an hour? Explain.

_____

18. A subway train has 8 cars that can each seat 55 people. What is the total number of people that can be seated on the train?

_____

## SCIENCE CONNECTION

19. In captivity, an Asian elephant needs about 875 pounds of food per week. A wild Asian elephant needs 2 times as much food plus 50 pounds more per day. About how many pounds of food does a wild Asian elephant need per day?

_____

20. A wild African elephant needs about 120 pounds more food per day than a wild Asian elephant. About how many pounds of food does a wild African elephant need per day?

_____

# Problem Solving

## DIVISION

**Solve each problem. Show your work.**

1. Duane has 12 times as many baseball cards as
   Tony. Between them, they have 208 baseball cards.
   How many baseball cards does each boy have?

   Tony
   Duane                                              208 baseball cards

2. Hallie has 10 times as many pages to read for her
   homework assignment as Janet. All together, they
   have to read 264 pages. How many pages does
   each girl have to read?

3. Hank has 48 fish in his aquarium. He has 11 times
   as many tetras as guppies. How many of each type
   of fish does Hank have?

4. Kelly has 4 times as many songs on her music
   player as Lou. Tiffany has 6 times as many songs
   on her music player as Lou. All together, they have
   682 songs on their music players. How many songs
   does Kelly have?

# Understanding Remainders

**Solve each word problem. Decide how the remainder affects the answer.**

1. Lana spent 96 hours knitting 19 shawls to sell at a crafts fair. If each shawl took about the same amount of time, how many hours did it take to knit each shawl?

   _____

2. Hal's Charter Service will have 72 customers for a fishing trip. Each boat can carry 13 passengers. How many boats will Hal need for the trip?

   _____

3. Raffle tickets cost $2.00 each. Ruth has $19.00. How many raffle tickets can she buy?

   _____

4. Helene has 384 yards of fabric. If each costume requires 11 yards of fabric, how many costumes can she make?

   _____

5. Neal bought 7 flashlights that use two size AA batteries. Batteries are sold in packs of 4. How many packs of batteries should he buy?

   _____

6. The chess club members baked 162 muffins for a school fundraiser. They packaged them in bags of 4 muffins. How many bags did they use? How many muffins were left unpackaged?

   _____

## MIXED APPLICATIONS

7. Ms. Sims's car travels 24 miles on 1 gallon of gas. One day she drove 126 miles. She started off with 9 gallons of gas in her car. Did she need to buy more gas for this trip? Explain.

   _____

8. A school cafeteria has 36 large tables that are all the same size. If 435 students eat in the cafeteria at the same time, can the same number of students sit at each table? Explain.

   _____

© Houghton Mifflin Harcourt Publishing Company

Name _____  Date _____

# The Coordinate Plane

There are six points plotted on the coordinate plane. You can use coordinates to name their location. For example, the coordinates (6, 4) name the location of Point *A*. Sometimes the coordinates are called an ordered pair. Use the coordinate plane for Exercises 1–9.

1. The *x*-axis and the *y*-axis of the coordinate plane meet to form a right angle. Circle the labels for the *x*- and *y*-axes, and circle where they meet, the origin.

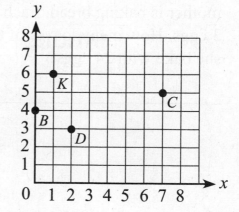

2. Start at the origin. To reach Point *A*, move _____ units to the right of the origin and _____ units up.

3. Describe how to reach Point *H* starting at the origin.

_____

4. What are the coordinates of Point *H*? (_____, _____)

5. Explain why a point's coordinates are sometimes called an ordered pair. (HINT: Think

of the meaning of the word *order*.) _____

**Write the coordinates for each point.**

6. Point *E* _____      7. Point *G* _____

8. Point *M* _____      9. Point *J* _____

**Name the point at each location.**

10. (0, 4) _____      11. (7, 5) _____

12. (2, 3) _____      13. (1, 6) _____

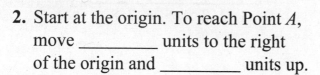

Name _____ Date _____

# Points on a Coordinate Plane

Use the coordinate plane for Exercises 1–12.

Write the ordered pair for each point.

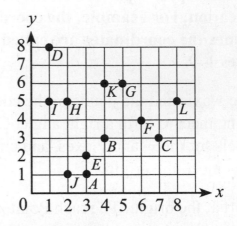

1. A _____
2. B _____
3. F _____
4. H _____
5. G _____
6. I _____
7. K _____
8. L _____

Name the point at each location.

9. (3, 2) _____
10. (7, 3) _____
11. (2, 1) _____
12. (1, 8) _____

## MIXED APPLICATIONS

13. On the coordinate plane above, if you move point E to the right 2 units and up 1 unit, what word will you spell?

_____

14. Gretel bought a carton of eggs for $1.79. She gave the clerk a $5 bill. How much change should she receive?

_____

15. Yoshi's family has chickens. His mother is baking bread. Each loaf uses 3 eggs. How many loaves of bread can she bake with 24 eggs?

_____

16. Yoshi is placing 78 eggs in cartons. He has 6-egg and 12-egg cartons. What is the smallest number of cartons he can use and still have every carton full?

_____

# Graphing Points on a Coordinate Plane

Use the coordinate plane for Exercises 1–12.

**Write the letter that names each point.**

**1.** (4, 2) _____  **2.** (9, 6) _____  **3.** (2, 1) _____

**4.** (8, 7) _____  **5.** (6, 4) _____  **6.** (10, 8) _____

**Write the coordinates for each point.**

**7.** A _____  **8.** V _____  **9.** N _____

**10.** E _____  **11.** F _____  **12.** I _____

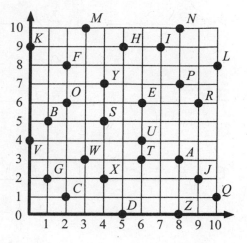

---

## MIXED APPLICATIONS

Use the coordinate plane above for Exercises 13–14.

**13.** Which points have a 5 as one of the coordinates? Write the points and their coordinates.

_____

_____

**14.** Spell a word using coordinates instead of letters. Challenge a friend to discover your word.

_____

_____

---

## LANGUAGE ARTS CONNECTION

**15.** Use the letters at the points to solve this riddle: What does the leopard say when it rains?

(5, 9) (4, 7) (6, 6) (5, 9)   (4, 7) (7, 8) (5, 9) (7, 3)

(5, 9) (4, 7) (8, 10)      (7, 3) (9, 1) (5, 0) (5, 9)

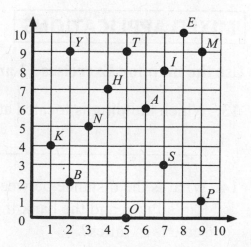

# Graph and Name Ordered Pairs

Use Coordinate Grid A to write an ordered pair for the given point.

**1.** A _____

**2.** B _____

**3.** C _____

**4.** D _____

**5.** E _____

**6.** F _____

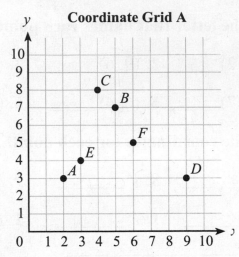

Coordinate Grid A

Plot and label the points on Coordinate Grid B.

**7.** N (7, 3)

**8.** R (0, 4)

**9.** O (8, 7)

**10.** M (2, 1)

**11.** P (5, 6)

**12.** Q (1, 5)

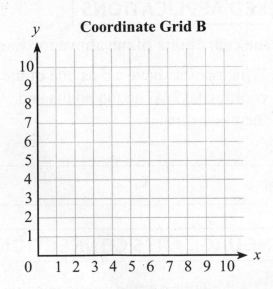

Coordinate Grid B

## MIXED APPLICATIONS

Use the map for Exercises 13 and 14.

**13.** Which building is located at (5, 6)?

_____

**14.** What is the distance between Kip's Pizza and the bank if the scale is in miles?

_____

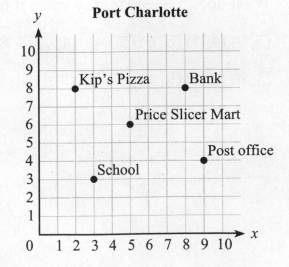

Port Charlotte

**70**

# Locations on a Coordinate Plane

Use the grid and the legend, or key, for Exercises 1–8.

Name the coordinates for each location.

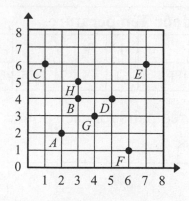

**1.** Barbara's house _____

**2.** Franco's house _____

**3.** Gloria's house _____

**4.** Hugo's house _____

| **LEGEND** | |
|---|---|
| *A* | Art's house |
| *B* | Barbara's house |
| *C* | Claire's house |
| *D* | Denny's house |
| *E* | Ellen's house |
| *F* | Franco's house |
| *G* | Gloria's house |
| *H* | Hugo's house |

Name the person whose house is at each of the following coordinates.

**5.** (2, 2) _____    **6.** (1, 6) _____

**7.** (7, 6) _____    **8.** (5, 4) _____

## MIXED APPLICATIONS

**9.** On grid paper, draw a grid like the one above. Plot points at (1, 1), (1, 3), (4, 3) and (4, 1). Connect the points in order to form a closed figure. What figure did you make?

_____

**10.** Sara has $20.00. She goes to the store and buys pencils for $2.00, books for $8.00, and a snack for $3.00. How much money does she have now?

_____

## ART CONNECTION

**11.** On a grid, draw a simple shape made up of line segments. Make a list of coordinates that, when connected, make the shape. Include any other instructions necessary. Give the list to a friend or family member. Have him or her use the coordinates to draw the shape.

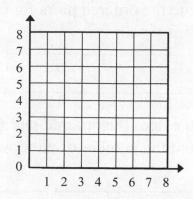

**Unit 7**
Core Skills Math, Grade 5

# Graph Data

**1.** Graph the data on the coordinate grid.

| Outdoor Temperature | | | | | |
|---|---|---|---|---|---|
| Hour | 1 | 3 | 5 | 7 | 9 |
| Temperature (°F) | 61 | 65 | 71 | 75 | 77 |

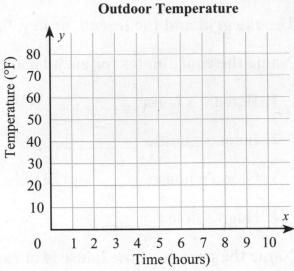

**Outdoor Temperature**

**2.** Write the ordered pairs for each point.

_____

_____

**3.** How would the ordered pairs be different if the outdoor temperature were recorded every hour for 4 consecutive hours?

_____

_____

## MIXED APPLICATIONS

**4.** Label the graph and then plot the data on the coordinate plane.

| Windows Repaired | | | | | |
|---|---|---|---|---|---|
| Day | 1 | 2 | 3 | 4 | 5 |
| Total Number Repaired | 14 | 30 | 45 | 63 | 79 |

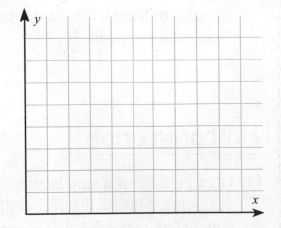

**5.** Write the ordered pairs for each point.

_____

_____

**6.** What does the ordered pair (2, 30) tell you about the number of windows repaired?

_____

# Line Graphs

Use the table for Exercises 1–5.

| Hourly Temperature | | | | | | | |
|---|---|---|---|---|---|---|---|
| Time | 10 A.M. | 11 A.M. | 12 noon | 1 P.M. | 2 P.M. | 3 P.M. | 4 P.M. |
| Temperature (°F) | 8 | 11 | 16 | 27 | 31 | 38 | 41 |

1. Write the related number pairs for the hourly temperature as ordered pairs.

_____

2. What scale would be appropriate to graph the temperature data?

_____

3. What interval would be appropriate to graph the temperature data?

_____

4. Make a line graph of the data.

_____

5. Use the graph to find the difference in temperature between 11 A.M. and 1 P.M.

_____

## MIXED APPLICATIONS

6. Between which two hours did the least change in temperature occur?

_____

7. What was the change in temperature between 12 noon and 4 P.M.?

_____

# Graph and Analyze Relationships

**Graph and label the related number pairs as ordered pairs. Then complete the rule and use it to find the unknown term.**

1. Multiply the number of yards by _____ to find the number of feet.

| Yards | 1 | 2 | 3 | 4 |
|-------|---|---|---|---|
| Feet  | 3 | 6 | 9 |   |

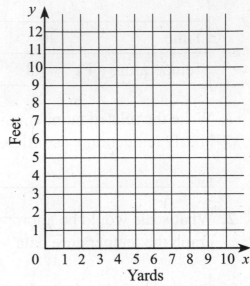

2. Multiply the number of quarts by _____ to find the number of cups that measure the same amount.

| Quarts | 1 | 2 | 3  | 4  | 5 |
|--------|---|---|----|----|---|
| Cups   | 4 | 8 | 12 | 16 |   |

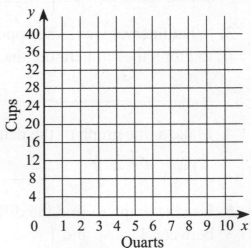

## MIXED APPLICATIONS

3. How can you use the graph for Exercise 2 to find how many cups are in 9 quarts?

_____

_____

_____

4. How many cups are equal to 9 quarts? _____

# Line Plots

**Use the data to complete the line plot. Then answer the questions.**

**A clerk in a health food store makes bags of trail mix. The amount of trail mix in each bag is listed below.**

$\frac{1}{4}$ lb, $\frac{1}{4}$ lb, $\frac{3}{4}$ lb, $\frac{1}{2}$ lb, $\frac{1}{4}$ lb, $\frac{3}{4}$ lb,

$\frac{3}{4}$ lb, $\frac{3}{4}$ lb, $\frac{1}{2}$ lb, $\frac{1}{4}$ lb, $\frac{1}{2}$ lb, $\frac{1}{2}$ lb

1. Write an addition sentence to find the combined weight of the $\frac{1}{4}$-lb bags. _____

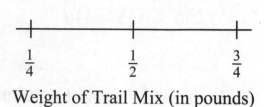

Weight of Trail Mix (in pounds)

2. What is the combined weight of the $\frac{1}{2}$-lb bags? _____

3. What is the combined weight of the $\frac{3}{4}$-lb bags? _____

4. What is the total weight of the trail mix used in all the bags? _____

5. What is the average amount of trail mix in each bag? _____

**Julie uses crystals to make a bracelet. The lengths of the crystals she uses are shown below. Use the data to complete the line plot.**

$\frac{1}{2}$ in., $\frac{5}{8}$ in., $\frac{3}{4}$ in., $\frac{1}{2}$ in., $\frac{3}{8}$ in., $\frac{1}{2}$ in., $\frac{3}{4}$ in.,

$\frac{3}{8}$ in., $\frac{3}{4}$ in., $\frac{5}{8}$ in., $\frac{1}{2}$ in., $\frac{3}{8}$ in., $\frac{5}{8}$ in., $\frac{3}{4}$ in.

6. What is the combined length of the $\frac{1}{2}$-in. crystals? _____

| | | | |
|---|---|---|---|
| $\frac{3}{8}$ | $\frac{1}{2}$ | $\frac{5}{8}$ | $\frac{3}{4}$ |

Lengths of Crystals (in inches)

7. What is the combined length of the $\frac{5}{8}$-in. crystals? _____

8. What is the total length of all the crystals in the bracelet? _____

9. What is the average length of each crystal in the bracelet? _____

# Using Mental Math to Multiply Decimals

**Use mental math to complete the pattern.**

**1.** $1 \times 0.13 = 0.13$

$10 \times 0.13 = n$

$100 \times 0.13 = 13$

$1,000 \times 0.13 = 130$

$n =$ _____

**2.** $1 \times 3.14 = 3.14$

$10 \times 3.14 = 31.4$

$100 \times 3.14 = n$

$1,000 \times 3.14 = 3,140$

$n =$ _____

**3.** $1 \times 42.3 = 42.3$

$10 \times 42.3 = 423$

$100 \times 42.3 = 4,230$

$1,000 \times 42.3 = n$

$n =$ _____

**Multiply each number by 10, 100, and 1,000.**

**4.** 0.3 _____

**5.** 6.2 _____

**6.** 8.04 _____

**7.** 1.31 _____

**Find each product.**

**8.** $10 \times 0.7 =$ _____

**9.** $100 \times 0.4 =$ _____

**10.** $10 \times 1.94 =$ _____

**11.** $100 \times 65.1 =$ _____

**12.** $10 \times 49.2 =$ _____

**13.** $100 \times 80.33 =$ _____

## MIXED APPLICATIONS

**14.** Rose can walk at a rate of 2.3 miles per hour. John can ride his bike at 10 times this rate. How far can John bike in an hour?

_____

**15.** Rosita can buy 50 recordable media CDs for $21.00. How much would she need to pay for 500 CDs at the same price?

_____

## EVERYDAY MATH CONNECTION

**16.** One country-western band sold 317 tickets to its first concert. They want to increase their ticket sales by at least ten times over the next two years. What is the minimum number of tickets they can sell for a concert to reach this goal?

_____

# Exploring Decimal Multiplication

**Multiply. Use the decimal model to help you.**

**1.**

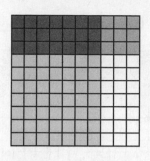

0.3 × 0.7 = _____

**2.**

0.2 × 0.3 = _____

**Make an area model to show each product.**

**3.**

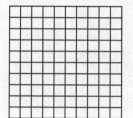

0.4 × 0.6 = _____

**4.**

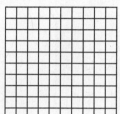

0.5 × 0.9 = _____

**5.**

0.5 × 0.7 = _____

**Use multiplication to find each product.**

**6.** 0.3 × 0.2 = _____      **7.** 0.6 × 0.3 = _____      **8.** 0.4 × 0.5 = _____

**9.** 0.8 × 0.9 = _____      **10.** 0.7 × 0.4 = _____      **11.** 0.1 × 0.9 = _____

## ART CONNECTION

**12.** In pottery making, a pot is formed from clay. Then it is dried, glazed, and fired (baked) in a very hot oven called a kiln. During firing, the wall of a pot can lose half of its thickness.

A potter wants to make a vase with a wall that is 0.4 inch thick. How thick should the wall be before the vase is fired?

_____

# Decimal Multiplication Using Models

**Multiply. Use the decimal model.**

**1.** $0.3 \times 0.6 =$ _____

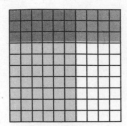

**2.** $0.2 \times 0.8 =$ _____

**3.** $0.5 \times 1.7 =$ _____

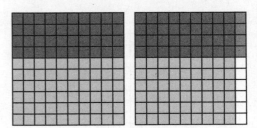

**4.** $0.6 \times 0.7 =$ _____

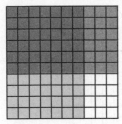

**5.** $0.8 \times 0.5 =$ _____

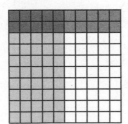

**6.** $0.4 \times 1.9 =$ _____

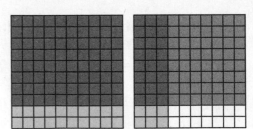

**7.** $0.8 \times 0.8 =$ _____

**8.** $0.2 \times 0.5 =$ _____

**9.** $0.8 \times 1.3 =$ _____

## MIXED APPLICATIONS

**10.** One type of bamboo plant grows 1.2 feet in 1 day. At that rate, how many feet could the plant grow in 0.5 day?

_____

**11.** The distance from the park to the grocery store is 0.9 mile. Ezra runs 8 tenths of that distance and walks the rest of the way. How far does Ezra run from the park to the grocery store?

_____

Unit 8
Core Skills Math, Grade 5

# Multiply Decimals and Whole Numbers Using a Model

**Use the decimal model to find the product.**

**1.** $4 \times 0.07 =$ _____

**2.** $3 \times 0.27 =$ _____

**3.** $2 \times 0.45 =$ _____

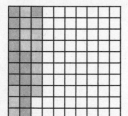
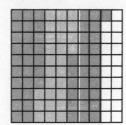

**Find the product. Draw a quick picture.**

**4.** $2 \times 0.8 =$ _____

**5.** $3 \times 0.33 =$ _____

**6.** $5 \times 0.71 =$ _____

**7.** $4 \times 0.23 =$ _____

---

## MIXED APPLICATIONS

**8.** In physical education class, Sonia walks a distance of 0.12 mile in 1 minute. At that rate, how far can she walk in 9 minutes?

_____

**9.** A certain tree can grow 0.45 meter in one year. At that rate, how much can the tree grow in 3 years?

_____

# Multiply Using Expanded Form

**Draw a model to find the product. Write the partial products inside the model.**

**1.** $37 \times 9.5 =$ _____

**2.** $84 \times 0.24 =$ _____

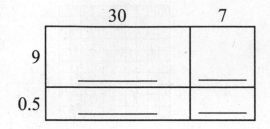

____ + ____ + ____ + ____ = ____

**Find the product.**

**3.** $13 \times 0.53 =$ _____

**4.** $27 \times 89.5 =$ _____

**5.** $32 \times 12.71 =$ _____

**6.** $17 \times 0.52 =$ _____

**7.** $23 \times 59.8 =$ _____

**8.** $61 \times 15.98 =$ _____

## MIXED APPLICATIONS

**9.** An object that weighs one pound on the moon would weigh about 6.02 pounds on Earth. Suppose a moon rock weighs 11 pounds on the moon. How much will it weigh on Earth?

_____

**10.** Tessa is on the track team. For practice and exercise, she runs 2.25 miles each day. At the end of 14 days, how many miles in all will Tessa have run?

_____

Name _____   Date _____

# Multiplying a Decimal by a Whole Number

**Write the product with the decimal point in the correct place.**

| **1.** | 5.2 | **2.** | 3.14 | **3.** | $6.13 | **4.** | $8.21 | **5.** | $6.85 |
|---|---|---|---|---|---|---|---|---|---|
| | × 7 | | × 8 | | × 13 | | × 21 | | × 63 |
| | 364 | | 2512 | | $7969 | | $17241 | | $43155 |

_____   _____   _____   _____   _____

**Estimate. Then find the product.**

| **6.** | 6.4 | **7.** | $12.31 | **8.** | 4.31 | **9.** | $4.99 | **10.** | 0.989 |
|---|---|---|---|---|---|---|---|---|---|
| | × 5 | | × 4 | | × 25 | | × 30 | | × 27 |

**11.** 4 × 12.6 = _____          **12.** 42 × $1.29 = _____

**13.** 9 × 1.034 = _____          **14.** 31 × 41.96 = _____

## MIXED APPLICATIONS

**15.** A marathon is about 26 miles in length, and 1 mile ≈ 1.609 kilometers. If a runner completes a marathon, how many kilometers does he or she run?

_____

**16.** A coffee shop pays $1.69 for a half-gallon of milk. If the shop uses 10 half-gallons a week, how much money will it spend on milk in 6 weeks?

_____

## SPORT CONNECTION

**17.** Write a word problem about a favorite sport or sports personality. The problem should require multiplying a decimal by a whole number to solve.

_____

_____

_____

**Unit 8**
Core Skills Math, Grade 5

# Multiplying Decimals

**Estimate first. Then find the product.**

1.    1.4
   × 0.7

2.    3.2
   × 0.9

3.    6.3
   × 3.7

4.    4.72
   × 6.2

5.    7.48
   × 5.3

6.    5.38
   × 7.6

7.    29.8
   × 4.4

8.    712.5
   × 0.16

9.    32.93
   × 3.7

10.    512.3
   × 2.7

11. $1.6 \times 0.8 =$ _____

12. $9.3 \times 4.2 =$ _____

13. $3.7 \times 6.8 =$ _____

14. $3.5 \times 4.17 =$ _____

15. $392.4 \times 2.7 =$ _____

16. $6.39 \times 2.6 =$ _____

**Compare. Write <, >, or =.**

17. $5.6 \times 3.8$ ◯ $5.1 \times 4.1$

18. $0.7 \times 8.3$ ◯ $4.1 \times 1.4$

19. $9.3 \times 1.6$ ◯ $16 \times 0.93$

20. $8.3 \times 4.9$ ◯ $5.7 \times 7.2$

## MIXED APPLICATIONS

21. One apple pie recipe has 160.15 calories per ounce. How many calories are in a slice of this pie that weighs 7.82 ounces?

_____

22. At Centerville Recycling, 13.62 tons of aluminum are recycled every month. How many tons of aluminum are recycled in 5 months?

_____

## MIXED REVIEW

**Multiply each number by 10, 100, and 1,000.**

23. 0.56 _____

24. 3.15 _____

25. 0.013 _____

**Estimate each product.**

26. $3.14 \times 9.8 \approx$ _____

27. $56 \times 3.91 \approx$ _____

28. $4.8 \times 13 \approx$ _____

Name _____  Date _____

# Zeros in the Product

**Write each product with the decimal point in the correct position. Write zeros if they are needed.**

| 1. | 0.03 | 2. | 0.08 | 3. | 0.06 | 4. | 0.05 |
|----|------|----|------|----|------|----|------|
| | × 0.6 | | × 0.5 | | × 1.1 | | × 0.4 |
| | 18 | | 40 | | 66 | | 20 |

_____  _____  _____  _____

**Find the product.**

| 5. | 0.04 | 6. | 0.46 | 7. | 2.07 | 8. | 4.02 |
|----|------|----|------|----|------|----|------|
| | × 0.9 | | × 0.2 | | × 6.5 | | × 1.5 |

9. $0.04 \times 25 =$ _____  10. $0.09 \times 0.1 =$ _____  11. $0.06 \times 0.4 =$ _____

12. $3.02 \times 0.5 =$ _____  13. $6.05 \times 0.2 =$ _____  14. $0.39 \times 2.2 =$ _____

## MIXED APPLICATIONS

15. What is the cost of 4 boxes of disks at Discount Disks?

_____

16. How much would you pay for 5 boxes of CDs at Computer City?

_____

| Price List – Disks and CDs | | |
|---|---|---|
| **Store** | **Box of Disks** | **Box of CDs** |
| Computers, Etc. | $3.99 | $10.29 |
| Software Plus | $2.79 | $10.29 |
| Computer City | $10.49 | $11.49 |
| Discount Disks | $6.89 | $4.79 |

## EVERYDAY MATH CONNECTION

17. Jason spends $8.27 on non-food items at the supermarket. The sales tax rate on these items is $0.05 per dollar. How much does Jason spend, including tax?

*Think:* $8.27 × _____ = _____, the tax on the items

_____ + _____ = _____, what Jason spent

# Using Mental Math to Divide Decimals

**Use mental math to complete each problem.**

**1.** 617 ÷ 10 = _____

617 ÷ 100 = 6.17

**2.** 4.8 ÷ 10 = 0.48

4.8 ÷ 100 = _____

**3.** 31.1 ÷ 10 = 3.11

31.1 ÷ 100 = _____

**Divide each number by 10, 100, and 1,000.**

**4.** 37 _____

**5.** 211 _____

**6.** 2,934 _____

**Find the quotient.**

**7.** 3.9 ÷ 10 = _____

**8.** 74 ÷ 10 = _____

**9.** 211 ÷ 100 = _____

**10.** 21.7 ÷ 100 = _____

**11.** 513 ÷ 100 = _____

**12.** 928 ÷ 1,000 = _____

**13.** 6.4 ÷ 10 = _____

**14.** 37 ÷ 10 = _____

**15.** 127 ÷ 100 = _____

**16.** 81.6 ÷ 100 = _____

**17.** 1,024 ÷ 100 = _____

**18.** 431 ÷ 1,000 = _____

## MIXED APPLICATIONS

**19.** Shawn has saved 5 pennies every day for the past year (365 days). How much money, in dollars, does he have now?

_____

**20.** Tonya donated $0.10 for every mile her friend Beth walked in the Walk for Hunger. If Beth walked 26.29 miles, how much did Tonya donate?

_____

## WRITER'S CORNER

**21.** Write two word problems that involve using mental math to divide a decimal. Choose any topics for your problems. Provide a solution.

_____

_____

_____

84

# Divide Decimals by Whole Numbers Using Models

**Use the model to complete the number sentence.**

**1.** 1.2 ÷ 4 = _____

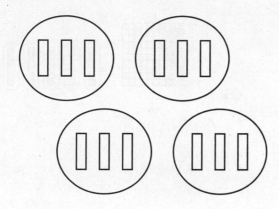

Each ⬜ = 0.1

**2.** 3.69 ÷ 3 = _____

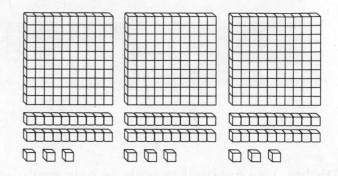

**3.** 4.9 ÷ 7 = _____     **4.** 3.6 ÷ 9 = _____     **5.** 2.4 ÷ 8 = _____

**6.** 6.48 ÷ 4 = _____     **7.** 3.01 ÷ 7 = _____     **8.** 4.26 ÷ 3 = _____

## MIXED APPLICATIONS

**9.** In PE class, Carl runs a distance of 1.17 miles in 9 minutes. At that rate, how far does Carl run in one minute?

_____

**10.** Marianne spends $9.45 on 5 greeting cards. Each card costs the same amount. What is the cost of one greeting card?

_____

Core Skills Math,

# Decimal Division

**Use the model to complete the number sentence**

**1.** 1.6 ÷ 0.4 = _____

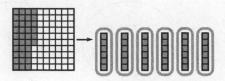

**2.** 0.36 ÷ 0.06 = _____

**Divide. Use decimal models to help you.**

**3.** 2.8 ÷ 0.7 = _____    **4.** 0.40 ÷ 0.05 = _____    **5** 0.45 ÷ 0.05 = _____

**6.** 1.62 ÷ 0.27 = _____    **7.** 0.56 ÷ 0.08 = _____    **8.** 1.8 ÷ 0.9 = _____

## MIXED APPLICATIONS

**9.** Keisha buys 2.4 kilograms of rice. She separates the rice into packages that contain 0.4 kilogram of rice each. How many packages of rice can Keisha make?

_____

**10.** Leighton is making cloth headbands. She has 4.2 yards of cloth. She uses 0.2 yard of cloth for each headband. How many headbands can Leighton make from the length of cloth she has?

_____

# Exploring Decimal Division

**Use base-ten blocks to help you.**

1. $2\overline{)3.14}$    2. $5\overline{)4.35}$    3. $3\overline{)6.18}$    4. $5\overline{)4.2}$    5. $2\overline{)3.7}$

6. $5\overline{)6.75}$    7. $6\overline{)4.20}$    8. $5\overline{)11.50}$    9. $3\overline{)5.25}$    10. $2\overline{)9.12}$

11. $7.36 \div 2 =$ _____    12. $6.15 \div 3 =$ _____    13. $7.92 \div 6 =$ _____

14. $6.68 \div 4 =$ _____    15. $2.04 \div 6 =$ _____    16. $4.56 \div 8 =$ _____

17. Kevin is building a doghouse. He bought 4 pieces of wood for the trim around the roof. If he paid $6.52 for the wood, how much did each piece cost?

_____

18. At ABC Hardware store, 6 size D batteries cost $8.34. Sesh has only $3.00. How many size D batteries can he buy? How much money will he have left?

_____

19. The corner store has fruit at these prices: apples, 6 for $4.44; pears, 4 for $4.32; and bananas, 5 for $1.65. How much will it cost Sonny to buy one of each fruit?

_____

20. Mr. Rivera hired 5 students to help him clean out his garage. He agreed to pay them $45.00. They did such a good job that he gave them the change in his pocket as a bonus, for a total of $49.35. How much did each student earn?

_____

## EVERYDAY MATH CONNECTION

21. Write a word problem that requires dividing a decimal by a whole number to solve it. Write the problem about the ingredients used in a favorite recipe.

_____

_____

_____

Name _____ Date _____

# Dividing Decimals by Whole Numbers

**Estimate the cost for one item.**

**1.** 12 eggs for $1.10 _____

**2.** 7 energy bars for $23.73 _____

**Find the quotient.**

**3.** $6\overline{)4.2}$

**4.** $7\overline{)2.8}$

**5.** $6\overline{)4.8}$

**6.** $9\overline{)0.27}$

**7.** $3\overline{)1.26}$

**8.** $5\overline{)5.25}$

**9.** $4\overline{)30.4}$

**10.** $7\overline{)9.17}$

**11.** $5\overline{)40.15}$

**12.** $6\overline{)44.4}$

**13.** $14\overline{)100.8}$

**14.** $21\overline{)277.2}$

**15.** $31\overline{)164.3}$

**16.** $68\overline{)0.816}$

**17.** $12\overline{)711.6}$

## MIXED APPLICATIONS

**Use the price list for Exercises 18 and 19.**

**18.** Find the cost of 5 pounds of flour and 2 loaves of bread.

_____

**19.** Estimate the cost of 1 pound of flour.

_____

| Price List | |
|---|---|
| half-gallon orange juice | $2.35 |
| 5-pound bag of flour | $2.19 |
| gallon of apple juice | $3.79 |
| quart of milk | $0.97 |
| loaf of bread | $0.79 |

## MIXED REVIEW

**Multiply.**

**20.** $0.05 \times 0.3 =$ _____

**21.** $0.15 \times 0.4 =$ _____

**22.** $4.02 \times 38 =$ _____

**Divide.**

**23.** $7.34 \div 10 =$ _____

**24.** $120 \div 100 =$ _____

**25.** $0.98 \div 10 =$ _____

# Exploring Mixed Numbers

**Write a mixed number or a whole number for each picture.**

1.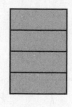

2.

3.

_____    _____    _____

**Rename each improper fraction as a mixed number or a whole number.**

4. $\dfrac{5}{4}$          5. $\dfrac{9}{5}$          6. $\dfrac{10}{6}$          7. $\dfrac{15}{5}$

_____    _____    _____    _____

**Rename each mixed number as an improper fraction.**

8. $4\dfrac{3}{8}$          9. $3\dfrac{1}{2}$          10. $2\dfrac{1}{3}$          11. $9\dfrac{3}{4}$

_____    _____    _____    _____

**Arrange in order from least to greatest.**

12. $3\dfrac{1}{4}, 3\dfrac{7}{8}, 3\dfrac{1}{3}$          13. $2\dfrac{1}{9}, 2\dfrac{3}{5}, 2\dfrac{1}{4}$

_____    _____

**Arrange in order from greatest to least.**

14. $1\dfrac{3}{5}, 1\dfrac{2}{3}, 1\dfrac{1}{5}$          15. $5\dfrac{4}{5}, 5\dfrac{1}{9}, 5\dfrac{3}{5}$

_____    _____

# Improper Fractions and Mixed Numbers

**Rename each improper fraction as a mixed number or a whole number.**

1. $\dfrac{24}{6}$ _____

2. $\dfrac{27}{9}$ _____

3. $\dfrac{30}{15}$ _____

4. $\dfrac{12}{12}$ _____

5. $\dfrac{13}{12}$ _____

6. $\dfrac{3}{2}$ _____

7. $\dfrac{4}{3}$ _____

8. $\dfrac{5}{4}$ _____

9. $\dfrac{11}{8}$ _____

10. $\dfrac{36}{6}$ _____

11. $\dfrac{7}{4}$ _____

12. $\dfrac{9}{3}$ _____

13. $\dfrac{64}{4}$ _____

14. $\dfrac{11}{5}$ _____

15. $\dfrac{16}{8}$ _____

**Rename each mixed number as an improper fraction.**

16. $4\dfrac{1}{2}$ _____

17. $5\dfrac{4}{5}$ _____

18. $6\dfrac{2}{3}$ _____

19. $7\dfrac{1}{4}$ _____

20. $2\dfrac{7}{10}$ _____

21. $8\dfrac{2}{9}$ _____

22. $17\dfrac{3}{5}$ _____

23. $9\dfrac{5}{8}$ _____

24. $4\dfrac{1}{6}$ _____

25. $2\dfrac{3}{5}$ _____

## MIXED REVIEW

**Write the fraction that names the shaded part of the model.**

26.

27.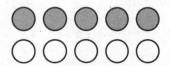

28.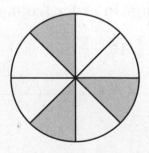

_____   _____   _____

**Write the fraction for the word name.**

29. three fifths _____

30. seven tenths _____

31. four sevenths _____

Unit 9
Core Skills Math, Grade 5

Name _____ Date _____

# Mixed Numbers and Fractions

**Find the missing digits.**

**1.** $\frac{7}{3} = 2\frac{\boxed{1}}{\boxed{\phantom{0}}}$ **2.** $\frac{29}{6} = \boxed{\phantom{0}}\frac{5}{6}$ **3.** $\frac{38}{5} = \boxed{\phantom{0}}\frac{3}{5}$ **4.** $9\frac{2}{3} = \frac{\boxed{\phantom{0}}}{3}$

**5.** $\frac{30}{7} = \boxed{\phantom{0}}\frac{2}{7}$ **6.** $\frac{14}{5} = 2\frac{\boxed{\phantom{0}}}{5}$ **7.** $11 = \frac{\boxed{\phantom{0}}}{4}$ **8.** $9 = \frac{\boxed{\phantom{0}}}{1}$

**Write the fraction as a mixed number or a whole number.**

**9.** $\frac{41}{8}$ _____ **10.** $\frac{7}{3}$ _____ **11.** $\frac{29}{11}$ _____ **12.** $\frac{15}{4}$ _____ **13.** $\frac{41}{9}$ _____

**14.** $\frac{27}{3}$ _____ **15.** $\frac{76}{12}$ _____ **16.** $\frac{81}{3}$ _____ **17.** $\frac{37}{14}$ _____ **18.** $\frac{47}{16}$ _____

**Write the mixed number as an improper fraction.**

**19.** $9\frac{1}{7}$ _____ **20.** $5\frac{7}{9}$ _____ **21.** $2\frac{3}{4}$ _____ **22.** $6\frac{2}{7}$ _____ **23.** $4\frac{9}{11}$ _____

**24.** $3\frac{3}{8}$ _____ **25.** $1\frac{9}{10}$ _____ **26.** $8\frac{1}{8}$ _____ **27.** $6\frac{7}{11}$ _____ **28.** $5\frac{4}{7}$ _____

## MIXED APPLICATIONS

**29.** I am a fraction that is greater than 1 but less than 2. The sum of my numerator and denominator is 11. My denominator subtracted from my numerator is 1. What fraction am I?

_____

**30.** Joy has $\frac{3}{4}$ cup of milk. She says that she has nine-sixteenths cup of milk. Is Joy correct? Explain.

_____

## MIXED REVIEW

**Find each product or quotient. Use mental math if possible.**

**31.** $6.2 \times 0.3 =$ _____ **32.** $0.7\overline{)2.45} =$ _____

**33.** $5\overline{)5.45} =$ _____ **34.** $0.78 \times 0.05 =$ _____

**Write the fraction in simplest form.**

**35.** $\frac{20}{25}$ _____ **36.** $\frac{2}{8}$ _____ **37.** $\frac{12}{36}$ _____ **38.** $\frac{10}{10}$ _____

91

# Interpret the Remainder

**Interpret the remainder to solve.**

1. Warren spent 140 hours making 16 wooden toy trucks for a craft fair. If he spent the same amount of time making each truck, how many hours did he spend making each truck?

_____

2. Marcia has 412 flowers for centerpieces. She uses 8 flowers in each centerpiece. How many centerpieces can she make?

_____

3. On the 5th grade class picnic, 50 students share 75 sandwiches equally. How many sandwiches does each student get?

_____

4. One plant container holds 14 tomato seedlings. If you have 1,113 seedlings, how many containers do you need to hold all the seedlings?

_____

## MIXED APPLICATIONS

5. Fiona bought 212 stickers to make a sticker book. If she places 18 stickers on each page, how many pages will her sticker book have?

_____

6. Jenny has 220 ounces of cleaning solution that she wants to divide equally among 12 large containers. How much cleaning solution should she put in each container?

_____

# Connect Fractions to Division

**Complete the number sentence to solve.**

**1.** Six students share 8 apples equally. How many apples does each student get?

$8 \div 6 =$ _____

**2.** Ten boys share 7 cereal bars equally. What fraction of a cereal bar does each boy get?

$7 \div 10 =$ _____

**3.** Eight friends share 12 tacos equally. How many tacos does each friend get?

$12 \div 8 =$ _____

**4.** Three girls share 8 yards of fabric equally. How many yards of fabric does each girl get?

$8 \div 3 =$ _____

**5.** Five bakers share 2 loaves of bread equally. What fraction of a loaf of bread does each baker get?

$2 \div 5 =$ _____

**6.** Nine friends share 6 fruit bars equally. What fraction of a fruit bar does each friend get?

$6 \div 9 =$ _____

**7.** Twelve students share 3 pears equally. What fraction of a pear does each student get?

$3 \div 12 =$ _____

**8.** Three sisters share 5 sandwiches equally. How many sandwiches does each sister get?

$5 \div 3 =$ _____

## MIXED APPLICATIONS

**9.** There are 12 students in a jewelry-making class and 8 sets of charms. What fraction of a set of charms will each student get?

_____

_____

**10.** Five friends share 6 packs of notecards equally. What part of the 6 packs will each friend get?

_____

_____

# Compare Fraction Factors and Products

**Complete each statement. Write *equal to*, *greater than*, or *less than*.**

**1.** $\frac{3}{5} \times \frac{4}{7}$ will be _____ $\frac{4}{7}$.

Think: $\frac{4}{7}$ is multiplied by a number less than 1.

**2.** $5 \times \frac{7}{8}$ will be _____ $\frac{7}{8}$.

**3.** $6 \times \frac{2}{5}$ will be _____ $\frac{2}{5}$.

**4.** $\frac{1}{9} \times 1$ will be _____ $\frac{1}{9}$.

**5.** $\frac{7}{8} \times \frac{3}{5}$ will be _____ $\frac{3}{5}$.

**6.** $\frac{4}{5} \times \frac{7}{7}$ will be _____ $\frac{4}{5}$.

## MIXED APPLICATIONS

**7.** Starla plans to multiply a recipe by 4. If the recipe calls for $\frac{1}{2}$ teaspoon vanilla extract, will she need more than $\frac{1}{2}$ teaspoon or less than $\frac{1}{2}$ teaspoon of vanilla extract?

_____

**8.** Miles is planning to spend $\frac{2}{3}$ as many hours bicycling this week as he did last week. Is Miles going to spend more hours or fewer hours bicycling this week than last week?

_____

Name _____ Date _____

# Compare Mixed Number Factors and Products

**Complete each statement. Write *equal to*, *greater than*, or *less than*.**

1. $\frac{2}{3} \times 1\frac{5}{8}$ will be _____ $1\frac{5}{8}$.  2. $\frac{5}{5} \times 2\frac{3}{4}$ will be _____ $2\frac{3}{4}$.

Think: $1\frac{5}{8}$ is multipled by a number less than 1.

3. $3 \times 3\frac{2}{7}$ will be _____ $3\frac{2}{7}$.  4. $9 \times 1\frac{4}{5}$ will be _____ $1\frac{4}{5}$.

5. $1\frac{7}{8} \times 2\frac{3}{8}$ will be _____ $2\frac{3}{8}$.  6. $3\frac{4}{9} \times \frac{5}{9}$ will be _____ $3\frac{4}{9}$.

---

**MIXED APPLICATIONS**

7. Fraser is making a scale drawing of a doghouse. The dimensions of the drawing will be $\frac{1}{8}$ of the dimensions of the actual doghouse. The height of the actual doghouse is $36\frac{3}{4}$ inches. Will the dimensions of Fraser's drawing be equal to, greater than, or less than the dimensions of the actual doghouse?

_____

8. Jorge has a recipe that calls for $2\frac{1}{3}$ cups of flour. He plans to make $1\frac{1}{2}$ times the recipe. Will the amount of flour Jorge needs be equal to, greater than, or less than the amount of flour his recipe calls for?

_____

**95**

© Houghton Mifflin Harcourt Publishing Company

Unit 9
Core Skills Math, Grade 5

# Unlike Fractions: Using Multiples

**Tell whether the second number is a multiple of the first number. Write *yes* or *no*.**

**1.** 6, 12 _____ **2.** 13, 26 _____ **3.** 8, 17 _____

**4.** 4, 9 _____ **5.** 6, 42 _____

**Tell whether one denominator is a multiple of the other. Write *yes* or *no*.**

**6.** $\frac{1}{5}, \frac{1}{10}$ _____ **7.** $\frac{3}{5}, \frac{1}{10}$ _____ **8.** $\frac{3}{4}, \frac{1}{5}$ _____ **9.** $\frac{2}{3}, \frac{3}{5}$ _____

**10.** $\frac{5}{10}, \frac{2}{5}$ _____ **11.** $\frac{3}{9}, \frac{5}{18}$ _____ **12.** $\frac{1}{12}, \frac{1}{5}$ _____ **13.** $\frac{5}{6}, \frac{7}{8}$ _____

**Use fraction bars or a sketch to find the sum or difference. Write the answer in simplest form.**

**14.** $\frac{1}{3} + \frac{1}{6} =$ _____ **15.** $\frac{5}{6} - \frac{1}{3} =$ _____ **16.** $\frac{7}{8} - \frac{3}{4} =$ _____

**17.** $\frac{9}{10} - \frac{1}{5} =$ _____ **18.** $\frac{2}{9} + \frac{1}{3} =$ _____ **19.** $\frac{3}{6} + \frac{1}{3} =$ _____

## EVERYDAY MATH CONNECTION

**Find each answer. Then write the answer in simplest form.**

**20.** There are 60 minutes in an hour. If Sandy takes 15 minutes to draw a picture, what part of an hour does she take?

_____

**21.** There are 60 seconds in a minute. Zack can run around the track in 50 seconds. What fraction of a minute is this?

_____

# Unlike Fractions: Least Common Denominator

**Find the least common multiple.**

**1.** 4, 16 _____  **2.** 2, 5 _____  **3.** 5, 15 _____  **4.** 6, 12 _____

**5.** 5, 3 _____  **6.** 3, 6 _____  **7.** 5, 9 _____  **8.** 4, 10 _____

**9.** 4, 12 _____  **10.** 9, 10 _____

**Find the least common denominator.**

**11.** $\frac{1}{5}, \frac{1}{3}$ _____  **12.** $\frac{1}{4}, \frac{4}{10}$ _____  **13.** $\frac{2}{9}, \frac{1}{6}$ _____  **14.** $\frac{3}{6}, \frac{1}{5}$ _____

**15.** $\frac{3}{8}, \frac{1}{5}$ _____  **16.** $\frac{2}{9}, \frac{1}{18}$ _____  **17.** $\frac{3}{7}, \frac{1}{5}$ _____  **18.** $\frac{1}{2}, \frac{7}{8}$ _____

**Use fractions bars to find each sum or difference. Write the answer in simplest form.**

**19.** $\frac{1}{3} + \frac{1}{2} =$ _____  **20.** $\frac{5}{6} + \frac{1}{12} =$ _____  **21.** $\frac{1}{6} + \frac{3}{4} =$ _____

## MUSIC CONNECTION

**22.** In $\frac{4}{4}$ time, one bar of music gets 4 beats, and a quarter note gets 1 beat. Since $\frac{1}{8}$ is one-half of $\frac{1}{4}$, an eighth note gets $\frac{1}{2}$ beat. Continue this relationship to complete the chart.

| | | |
|---|---|---|
| **Quarter note** | ♩ | = 1 beat |
| **Eighth note** | ♪ | = $\frac{1}{2}$ beat |
| **Sixteenth note** | ♬ | = _____ beat |
| **Thirty-second note** | ♪ | = _____ beat |

# Adding and Subtracting Using Multiples

**Complete. Use fraction pieces and multiples to help you.**

1. $\frac{7}{10} \rightarrow$ ☐/☐

   $-\frac{1}{2} \rightarrow$ ☐/☐

   ☐/☐

2. $\frac{1}{9} \rightarrow$ ☐/☐

   $+\frac{1}{3} \rightarrow$ ☐/☐

   ☐/☐

3. $\frac{5}{8} \rightarrow$ ☐/☐

   $+\frac{1}{4} \rightarrow$ ☐/☐

   ☐/☐

4. $\frac{10}{16} \rightarrow$ ☐/☐

   $-\frac{5}{8} \rightarrow$ ☐/☐

   ☐/☐

## MIXED APPLICATIONS

5. Alan is making a fruit cup for desert. He needs $\frac{3}{4}$ cup of pineapple. He has $\frac{1}{2}$ cup of pineapple. How many cups of pineapple does he still need?

   _____

6. Alan uses $\frac{1}{4}$ cup of pecans to make nut bread and $\frac{3}{8}$ cup to make trail mix. How many cups of pecans does he use in all?

   _____

## EVERYDAY MATH CONNECTION

7. Umeko has only a $\frac{1}{4}$-cup measuring cup. She needs to measure several quantities of flour. Complete the table to tell how many times she will need to fill her $\frac{1}{4}$-cup measure to get the given number of cups of flour.

| Flour Needed | $\frac{1}{2}$ c | 1 c | $1\frac{1}{4}$ c | 2 c | $3\frac{1}{2}$ c | $5\frac{3}{4}$ c |
|---|---|---|---|---|---|---|
| Number of $\frac{1}{4}$-cups needed | | | | | | |

# Adding and Subtracting Using Least Common Denominator

**Fill in the missing digits to write an equivalent fraction. Then add or subtract.**

1.  $\dfrac{2}{3} = \dfrac{\boxed{\phantom{0}}}{12}$

    $+ \dfrac{1}{4} = \dfrac{\boxed{\phantom{0}}}{12}$

    $\dfrac{\boxed{\phantom{0}}}{12}$

2.  $\dfrac{4}{5} = \dfrac{8}{\boxed{\phantom{0}}}$

    $- \dfrac{1}{2} = \dfrac{5}{\boxed{\phantom{0}}}$

    $\dfrac{3}{\boxed{\phantom{0}}}$

3.  $\dfrac{2}{6} = \dfrac{\boxed{\phantom{0}}}{\boxed{\phantom{0}}}$

    $+ \dfrac{2}{5} = \dfrac{\boxed{\phantom{0}}}{\boxed{\phantom{0}}}$

    $\dfrac{\boxed{\phantom{0}}}{\boxed{\phantom{0}}} = \dfrac{11}{15}$

**Write an equivalent fraction using the least common denominator. Find the sum or difference in simplest form.**

4.  $\dfrac{1}{2}$
    $+ \dfrac{1}{8}$
    _____

5.  $\dfrac{4}{5}$
    $- \dfrac{2}{3}$
    _____

6.  $\dfrac{2}{6}$
    $+ \dfrac{3}{10}$
    _____

7.  $\dfrac{3}{4}$
    $- \dfrac{3}{8}$
    _____

8.  $\dfrac{2}{5}$
    $+ \dfrac{2}{4}$
    _____

## MIXED APPLICATIONS

9.  Whit lives $\dfrac{5}{8}$ mile from his office. He usually drives on the expressway. If traffic is bad, he takes a different route that is $\dfrac{7}{8}$ mile long. How much shorter is his drive if he goes on the expressway?

    _____

10. Sonja is baking. She needs $\dfrac{1}{4}$ teaspoon salt for dinner rolls, $\dfrac{1}{8}$ teaspoon salt for muffins, and $\dfrac{1}{2}$ teaspoon salt for bread. How many teaspoons of salt does she need in all?

    _____

## NUMBER SENSE

11. Jennifer needs these quantities of ribbon: $\dfrac{1}{8}$ yard red, $\dfrac{1}{4}$ yard blue, and $\dfrac{1}{2}$ yard green. She estimates that she needs about $\dfrac{1}{2}$ yard of ribbon in all. Is this a good estimate? Explain in terms of the exact answer.

_____

**99**

# Adding and Subtracting Unlike Fractions

**Add or subtract. Write the answer in simplest form.**

1.  $\begin{array}{r} \frac{1}{3} \\ + \frac{1}{5} \\ \hline \end{array}$

2.  $\begin{array}{r} \frac{1}{2} \\ + \frac{1}{5} \\ \hline \end{array}$

3.  $\begin{array}{r} \frac{4}{5} \\ - \frac{1}{4} \\ \hline \end{array}$

4.  $\begin{array}{r} \frac{2}{3} \\ + \frac{1}{6} \\ \hline \end{array}$

5.  $\begin{array}{r} \frac{7}{8} \\ - \frac{1}{2} \\ \hline \end{array}$

6.  $\begin{array}{r} \frac{1}{2} \\ - \frac{1}{4} \\ \hline \end{array}$

7.  $\begin{array}{r} \frac{7}{10} \\ - \frac{2}{5} \\ \hline \end{array}$

8.  $\begin{array}{r} \frac{1}{5} \\ + \frac{1}{4} \\ \hline \end{array}$

9.  $\begin{array}{r} \frac{1}{6} \\ + \frac{1}{2} \\ \hline \end{array}$

10.  $\begin{array}{r} \frac{1}{4} \\ - \frac{1}{5} \\ \hline \end{array}$

11. $\frac{2}{3} + \frac{1}{5} =$ _____

12. $\frac{7}{8} - \frac{1}{4} =$ _____

13. $\frac{3}{7} + \frac{1}{2} =$ _____

14. $\frac{1}{8} + \frac{1}{4} =$ _____

15. $\frac{1}{4} + \frac{5}{12} =$ _____

16. $\frac{2}{3} - \frac{1}{6} =$ _____

## MIXED APPLICATIONS

17. A dressmaker has $\frac{3}{8}$ yard of fabric. She needs a total of $\frac{3}{4}$ yard for a skirt. How much more fabric does she need?

_____

18. John is making a shelf that requires $\frac{7}{8}$ foot of lumber. He has $\frac{1}{2}$ foot of lumber. How much more lumber does he need?

_____

## MIXED REVIEW

**Order each set of numbers from least to greatest.**

19. $\frac{5}{8}, \frac{3}{4}, \frac{2}{3}$ _____

20. $\frac{5}{6}, \frac{1}{2}, \frac{4}{9}$ _____

21. $\frac{8}{9}, \frac{1}{3}, \frac{5}{12}$ _____

22. 0.050, 0.005, 0.505 _____

23. 4.123; 41,230; 41.23 _____

# Exploring Adding Mixed Numbers

**Estimate the sum.**

1. $4\frac{3}{4}$
   $+ 2\frac{3}{8}$
   _____

2. $6\frac{7}{8}$
   $+ 1\frac{1}{4}$
   _____

3. $2\frac{1}{4}$
   $+ 2\frac{3}{4}$
   _____

4. $6\frac{1}{4}$
   $+ 2\frac{1}{8}$
   _____

5. $5\frac{1}{3}$
   $+ 1\frac{1}{6}$
   _____

6. $4\frac{1}{5}$
   $+ 2\frac{2}{5}$
   _____

7. $6\frac{1}{4}$
   $+ 1\frac{1}{2}$
   _____

8. $7\frac{5}{6}$
   $+ 3\frac{1}{6}$
   _____

9. $4\frac{2}{7}$
   $+ 1\frac{3}{7}$
   _____

10. $5\frac{1}{3}$
    $+ 3\frac{1}{8}$
    _____

**Decide whether you need to rename the fraction to write the sum in simplest form. Write *yes* or *no*.**

11. $8\frac{1}{6}$
    $+ 1\frac{5}{6}$
    _____

12. $3\frac{3}{8}$
    $+ 2\frac{7}{8}$
    _____

13. $5\frac{2}{7}$
    $+ 3\frac{6}{7}$
    _____

14. $7\frac{2}{5}$
    $+ 4\frac{1}{5}$
    _____

15. $3\frac{1}{3}$
    $+ 2\frac{2}{3}$
    _____

_____   _____   _____   _____   _____

**Use fraction strips to find the sum in simplest form.**

16. $3\frac{3}{4}$
    $+ 1\frac{1}{8}$
    _____

17. $3\frac{3}{4}$
    $+ 2\frac{3}{4}$
    _____

18. $4\frac{3}{4}$
    $+ 3\frac{1}{8}$
    _____

19. $3\frac{7}{8}$
    $+ 2\frac{1}{8}$
    _____

20. $3\frac{2}{3}$
    $+ 1\frac{1}{6}$
    _____

21. $3\frac{1}{10}$
    $+ 2\frac{3}{5}$
    _____

---

**MIXED REVIEW**

**Multiply or divide. Use mental math when possible.**

22. $25$
    $\times 60$

23. $35$
    $\times 43$

24. $32$
    $\times 28$

25. $2\overline{)424}$

26. $5\overline{)250}$

27. $6\overline{)318}$

# Adding Mixed Numbers

**Estimate the sum.**

1. $4\frac{5}{12}$
   $+ 3\frac{2}{12}$
   _____

2. $8\frac{1}{10}$
   $+ 1\frac{7}{10}$
   _____

3. $5\frac{2}{5}$
   $+ 2\frac{1}{15}$
   _____

4. $1\frac{5}{9}$
   $+ 2\frac{1}{3}$
   _____

5. $8\frac{2}{3}$
   $+ 7\frac{3}{7}$
   _____

**Find the sum. Write the answer in simplest form.**

6. $7\frac{3}{10}$
   $+ 7\frac{5}{10}$
   _____

7. $2\frac{1}{9}$
   $+ 5\frac{5}{9}$
   _____

8. $3\frac{3}{13}$
   $+ 2\frac{5}{13}$
   _____

9. $3\frac{4}{8}$
   $+ 9\frac{2}{8}$
   _____

10. $1\frac{2}{6}$
    $+ 8\frac{3}{6}$
    _____

11. $4\frac{11}{15}$
    $+ 5\frac{2}{3}$
    _____

12. $12\frac{2}{3}$
    $+ 4\frac{2}{9}$
    _____

13. $5\frac{1}{3}$
    $+ 4\frac{3}{8}$
    _____

14. $3\frac{6}{7}$
    $+ 4\frac{1}{4}$
    _____

15. $4\frac{1}{2}$
    $+ 3\frac{1}{3}$
    _____

16. $14\frac{2}{5} + 3\frac{1}{3} =$ _____

17. $11\frac{4}{9} + 8\frac{1}{4} =$ _____

18. $17\frac{2}{9} + 2\frac{5}{8} =$ _____

## MIXED APPLICATIONS

19. A plumber bought two pipes. One was $3\frac{1}{4}$ feet long, and the other was $2\frac{5}{8}$ feet long. What is the total length of the pipe purchased?

_____

20. Patrick worked in the kennel for $4\frac{2}{5}$ hours on Friday and $6\frac{3}{10}$ hours on Saturday. How many hours in all did he work?

_____

## NUMBER SENSE

21. There are two identical grain silos on Gabriel's farm. One is $\frac{1}{7}$ full and the other is $\frac{4}{21}$ full. Gabriel wants to put all of the grain into one silo. Will the silo be full? Explain.

_____

# Subtracting Mixed Numbers: Vertical

**Use fraction strips or circles to find the difference in simplest form.**

1. $2\frac{1}{3}$
$-\ 1\frac{2}{3}$
_____

2. $3\frac{3}{5}$
$-\ \ \ \frac{4}{5}$
_____

3. $4\frac{1}{4}$
$-\ 2\frac{3}{4}$
_____

4. $3\frac{4}{9}$
$-\ 1\frac{8}{9}$
_____

5. $5\frac{6}{11}$
$-\ 2\frac{9}{11}$
_____

6. $5\frac{2}{5}$
$-\ 1\frac{4}{5}$
_____

7. $6$
$-\ 2\frac{1}{3}$
_____

8. $2\frac{3}{7}$
$-\ \ \ \frac{6}{7}$
_____

9. $8$
$-\ 3\frac{1}{8}$
_____

10. $3\frac{1}{9}$
$-\ 1\frac{8}{9}$
_____

**Decide whether you need to rename to subtract. Write *yes* or *no*.**

11. $10\frac{1}{2}$
$-\ 7\frac{1}{2}$
_____

12. $8\frac{2}{5}$
$-\ 5\frac{3}{5}$
_____

13. $2\frac{5}{8}$
$-\ 1\frac{1}{8}$
_____

14. $2\frac{3}{8}$
$-\ \ \ \frac{1}{8}$
_____

15. $3$
$-\ 2\frac{1}{3}$
_____

**Estimate. If the estimate is greater than 2, find the actual difference.**

16. $7\frac{1}{5}$
$-\ 3\frac{4}{5}$
_____

17. $4$
$-\ 2\frac{1}{2}$
_____

18. $6\frac{1}{3}$
$-\ 1\frac{2}{3}$
_____

19. $5\frac{2}{5}$
$-\ 3\frac{3}{5}$
_____

20. $5\frac{3}{8}$
$-\ 2\frac{1}{8}$
_____

## PHYSICAL EDUCATION CONNECTION

21. Dieter won the high jump event by jumping $7\frac{3}{4}$ feet. Allen jumped $6\frac{1}{4}$ feet. How much higher was Dieter's winning jump?

_____

**103**

Name _____   Date _____

# Subtracting Mixed Numbers: Horizontal

**1.** Is it necessary to rename if you are subtracting $4\frac{2}{3} - 2\frac{1}{3}$? Justify your answer.

_____

**2.** Is it necessary to rename if you are subtracting $5\frac{2}{5} - 1\frac{4}{5}$? Justify your answer.

_____

**Tell whether or not you need to rename the larger number. Then rename if necessary.**

**3.**  $3\frac{2}{7}$    **4.**   $5\frac{6}{10}$    **5.**   $3\frac{2}{5}$    **6.**   $4\frac{7}{8}$    **7.**   $1\frac{10}{11}$    **8.**   $2\frac{2}{9}$

   $- 1\frac{5}{7}$      $- 2\frac{2}{10}$      $- 1\frac{3}{5}$      $- 3\frac{1}{8}$      $- \frac{6}{11}$      $- 1\frac{4}{9}$

   _____     _____     _____     _____     _____     _____

**Rename the larger number.**

**9.** $3 - 1\frac{3}{5}$ _____

**10.** $3\frac{1}{7} - 1\frac{2}{7}$ _____

**11.** $4\frac{5}{8} - 2\frac{7}{8}$ _____

**12.** $6 - 2\frac{3}{4}$ _____

**13.** $7\frac{3}{13} - 5\frac{7}{13}$ _____

**14.** $8\frac{2}{15} - 6\frac{11}{15}$ _____

**Find the difference.**

**15.** $8 - 5\frac{3}{4} =$ _____

**16.** $12 - 10\frac{2}{3} =$ _____

**17.** $8\frac{1}{4} - 6\frac{3}{4} =$ _____

**18.** $6\frac{1}{6} - 4\frac{5}{6} =$ _____

**19.** $4\frac{1}{9} - 2\frac{5}{9} =$ _____

**20.** $5\frac{5}{12} - 3\frac{7}{12} =$ _____

**21.** $8\frac{1}{7} - 2\frac{5}{7} =$ _____

**22.** $9 - 6\frac{6}{7} =$ _____

**23.** $20 - 12\frac{5}{9} =$ _____

**24.** $7\frac{3}{8} - 3\frac{7}{8} =$ _____

**25.** $11 - 7\frac{1}{6} =$ _____

**26.** $18 - 11\frac{3}{5} =$ _____

**NUMBER SENSE**

**27.** Two fractions have a sum of $\frac{5}{6}$. Their difference is $\frac{1}{6}$. What are the fractions?

_____

**104**

   Core Skills Math, Grade 5

# Renaming Mixed Numbers

**Estimate each sum or difference.**

1. $5\frac{3}{4} + 6\frac{1}{12} \approx$ _____

2. $8\frac{1}{2} - 4\frac{7}{8} \approx$ _____

3. $5\frac{2}{3} + 4\frac{1}{3} \approx$ _____

4. $2\frac{1}{3} - 1\frac{1}{12} \approx$ _____

5. $12\frac{1}{16} + 4\frac{1}{4} \approx$ _____

6. $8\frac{7}{8} - 5\frac{1}{2} \approx$ _____

**Add or subtract. Write each answer in simplest form.**

7. $\begin{aligned} 9\frac{1}{6} \\ - 8\frac{2}{3} \end{aligned}$
8. $\begin{aligned} 9\frac{4}{5} \\ + 2\frac{3}{10} \end{aligned}$
9. $\begin{aligned} 8\frac{5}{9} \\ + 6\frac{2}{3} \end{aligned}$
10. $\begin{aligned} 5\frac{1}{3} \\ - 3\frac{4}{9} \end{aligned}$
11. $\begin{aligned} 7\frac{4}{5} \\ + 8\frac{7}{20} \end{aligned}$

12. $\begin{aligned} 5\frac{1}{4} \\ - 2\frac{11}{12} \end{aligned}$
13. $\begin{aligned} 8\frac{5}{6} \\ + 3\frac{1}{3} \end{aligned}$
14. $\begin{aligned} 2\frac{1}{4} \\ - 1\frac{5}{8} \end{aligned}$
15. $\begin{aligned} 8\frac{6}{7} \\ - 2\frac{13}{14} \end{aligned}$
16. $\begin{aligned} 5\frac{2}{3} \\ + 3\frac{5}{6} \end{aligned}$

17. $\begin{aligned} 4\frac{2}{3} \\ - 2\frac{3}{4} \end{aligned}$
18. $\begin{aligned} 6\frac{1}{6} \\ + 1\frac{11}{12} \end{aligned}$
19. $\begin{aligned} 5\frac{3}{8} \\ + 2\frac{3}{4} \end{aligned}$
20. $\begin{aligned} 9\frac{1}{9} \\ - 4\frac{2}{3} \end{aligned}$
21. $\begin{aligned} 5\frac{8}{9} \\ + 8\frac{1}{6} \end{aligned}$

## MIXED APPLICATIONS

22. Lana worked for $3\frac{3}{4}$ hours on Monday and $6\frac{1}{2}$ hours on Tuesday. How many hours did she work in all?

_____

23. Joe has a $15\frac{5}{6}$ ft piece of wood. He uses $11\frac{2}{3}$ ft for a project. How much wood is left?

_____

## HEALTH CONNECTION

24. A pamphlet about diet states that the average person should eat $\frac{9}{2}$ cups of fruits and vegetables a day, excluding potatoes. How many cups is this in simplest form?

_____

**105**

# Exploring Subtraction of Mixed Numbers

**You need to subtract $2\frac{2}{3} - 1\frac{3}{4}$.**

1. Do you need to write equivalent fractions using the least common denominator (LCD)? Explain your answer.

   _____

2. Do you need to rename the mixed numbers? Justify your answer.

   _____

**You need to subtract $4\frac{3}{5} - 3\frac{4}{5}$.**

3. Do you need to write equivalent fractions using the least common denominator (LCD)? Explain your answer.

   _____

4. Do you need to rename the mixed numbers? Justify your answer.

   _____

**Use the LCD to rename fractions, if necessary. Then tell whether you need to rename the mixed number before you can subtract.**

5. $3\frac{1}{6} - \frac{5}{6}$ _____

6. $4\frac{3}{4} - 2\frac{1}{2}$ _____

7. $5\frac{4}{7} - 1\frac{2}{5}$ _____

8. $3\frac{1}{5} - 1\frac{4}{5}$ _____

9. $1\frac{2}{3} - \frac{1}{15}$ _____

10. $1\frac{4}{7} - \frac{5}{7}$ _____

**Find the difference. Write the answer in simplest form.**

11. $2\frac{1}{4} - \frac{3}{4} =$ _____

12. $5\frac{1}{6} - 3\frac{7}{12} =$ _____

13. $11\frac{4}{5} - 7\frac{1}{2} =$ _____

14. $8\frac{6}{7} - 3\frac{1}{14} =$ _____

15. $15\frac{2}{9} - 5\frac{1}{3} =$ _____

16. $5\frac{1}{5} - 1\frac{1}{4} =$ _____

17. $4\frac{3}{4} - 2\frac{9}{10} =$ _____

18. $19\frac{1}{7} - 4\frac{2}{3} =$ _____

19. $21\frac{1}{2} - 18\frac{5}{6} =$ _____

### WRITER'S CORNER

20. Write a word problem that involves subtracting two mixed numbers with unlike denominators.

   _____

   _____

**106**

# Subtracting Mixed Numbers with Unlike Denominators

**Estimate the difference.**

1. $5\frac{1}{7} - 2\frac{3}{4} \approx$ _____

2. $8\frac{1}{3} - 4\frac{1}{5} \approx$ _____

3. $4\frac{8}{9} - 1\frac{1}{2} \approx$ _____

**Find the difference. Write the answer in simplest form.**

4. $8\frac{5}{6}$
   $- 3\frac{1}{3}$

5. $8\frac{3}{7}$
   $- 3\frac{1}{4}$

6. $5\frac{6}{10}$
   $- 1\frac{1}{5}$

7. $7\frac{2}{3}$
   $- 2\frac{1}{4}$

8. $9\frac{3}{7}$
   $- 2\frac{1}{2}$

9. $19\frac{1}{5}$
   $- 12\frac{2}{3}$

10. $21\frac{4}{7}$
    $- 16\frac{1}{3}$

11. $27\frac{1}{3}$
    $- 12\frac{3}{8}$

12. $33\frac{1}{2}$
    $- 22\frac{5}{6}$

13. $45\frac{2}{3}$
    $- 25\frac{9}{10}$

14. $14\frac{1}{5} - 3\frac{5}{15} =$ _____

15. $18\frac{3}{4} - 12\frac{7}{9} =$ _____

16. $35\frac{1}{2} - 31\frac{4}{7} =$ _____

## MIXED APPLICATIONS

17. Rusty bought some shares of stock when its value was up $23\frac{3}{8}$ points. A week later it had dropped to $19\frac{3}{4}$ points. How much did the stock drop?

18. Clint is a wrestler. He weighs $143\frac{1}{4}$ pounds and his opponent weighs $141\frac{1}{2}$ pounds. By how much does Clint outweigh his opponent?

## NUMBER SENSE

19. The sum of two numbers is $8\frac{1}{6}$. One of the numbers is $2\frac{2}{3}$. What is the other number?

20. The sum of two numbers is 9. One number is $4\frac{6}{7}$. What is the other number?

Unit 10
Core Skills Math, Grade 5

# Problem Solving

## FRACTIONS

**Find the answer in simplest form and show your work.**

1. About one third of the town's residents have the newspaper delivered. What fraction of the residents do not have the newspaper delivered?

_____

2. Ann lives $\frac{3}{10}$ mile from school. Carlos lives $\frac{1}{10}$ mile from school. How much farther from school does Ann live than Carlos?

_____

3. Antonio roped off a square section of the park for a picnic. He used $15\frac{1}{2}$ feet of rope on each side. How much rope did he use in all?

_____

4. Two prize-winning fish in the annual freshwater fishing tournament weighed $11\frac{1}{2}$ pounds and $12\frac{1}{16}$ pounds. How much did they weigh altogether?

_____

5. The clerk in a fabric store cuts $7\frac{7}{8}$ yards of fabric from a bolt containing $26\frac{5}{8}$ yards of fabric. How much fabric is left on the bolt?

_____

6. Tamara bought two bottles of perfume. One bottle contains $\frac{1}{2}$ ounce. The other contains $1\frac{3}{4}$ ounces. How much perfume did Tamara buy in all?

_____

7. Two of the wettest cities in the continental United States receive about $62\frac{2}{10}$ inches and $61\frac{9}{10}$ inches of rain per year. How much rain do the two cities receive in all each year?

_____

8. Donna's upper arm bone, or humerus, is $36\frac{1}{2}$ centimeters long. One of her lower arm bones, the ulna, is $28\frac{1}{5}$ centimeters long. What is the combined length of these two bones?

_____

**108**

# Problem Solving

## APPLICATIONS

**Find the answer in simplest form and show your work.**

1. The results of a survey showed that seven tenths of the households surveyed used a computer. What fraction of the households surveyed did not use a computer?

_____

2. A standard sheet of paper measures $8\frac{1}{2}$ inches by 11 inches. How much longer is the paper than it is wide?

_____

3. The first-place finisher in a high school long jump event recorded a jump of $18\frac{3}{4}$ feet. The second place jump was $\frac{1}{2}$ foot shorter. What was the recorded second-place jump?

_____

4. For Thanksgiving, Joe's family cooked a $17\frac{1}{2}$-pound turkey. Diana's family cooked a $22\frac{1}{4}$-pound turkey. How much more did the larger turkey weigh than the smaller one?

_____

5. The Jubilee Diamond is considered the world's most perfectly cut diamond. It weighs $245\frac{1}{3}$ carats. The more famous Hope Diamond weighs $45\frac{1}{5}$ carats. What is the difference in the weights of the two diamonds?

_____

6. Sam, Laura, and Gina live outside of the city. Sam lives 5 miles from the city limits. Laura lives $\frac{3}{4}$ mile closer than Sam does. Gina lives $\frac{1}{2}$ mile closer than Laura does. How far from the city limits does Gina live?

_____

7. In the spring of one year, East Hill Farm received $7\frac{7}{10}$ inches of rain. The following spring it received $4\frac{1}{2}$ inches less rain. How much rain did the farm receive the following spring?

_____

8. Sue needs to put molding along a 46-inch section of wall. She has a $28\frac{1}{2}$-inch piece and a $23\frac{3}{4}$-inch piece of molding. What length piece can she cut from the shorter piece so the longer pieces added together will total 46 inches?

_____

**109**

# Multiplying Fractions and Whole Numbers

**Write a number sentence for each picture. Show a fraction multiplied by a whole number and their product.**

1.

2.

3.

_____      _____      _____

**Multiply. Write the product as a whole or mixed number.**

4. $\frac{1}{3} \times 9 =$ _____

5. $\frac{1}{4} \times 32 =$ _____

6. $\frac{3}{5} \times 5 =$ _____

7. $\frac{3}{4} \times 12 =$ _____

8. $\frac{1}{5} \times 20 =$ _____

9. $\frac{1}{3} \times 7 =$ _____

10. $\frac{4}{5} \times 2 =$ _____

11. $\frac{1}{3} \times 21 =$ _____

12. $\frac{5}{8} \times 10 =$ _____

13. $12 \times \frac{1}{3} =$ _____

14. $\frac{3}{5} \times 8 =$ _____

15. $\frac{3}{4} \times 3 =$ _____

## MIXED APPLICATIONS

16. The band is selling 500 boxes of granola bars as a fundraiser. They have sold $\frac{3}{5}$ of the boxes. How many boxes are left to sell?

17. Each box of granola bars sold increases the fund by $2.25. Carmen sold 75 boxes. How much money did Carmen's sales add to the fund?

## SOCIAL STUDIES CONNECTION

18. In the United States, presidential elections are determined by electoral votes. Each state receives one vote for each of its two senators and one vote for each of its representatives in Congress. Washington, D.C., has three electoral votes. Currently, the total number of electoral votes is 538. If a state casts about $\frac{1}{18}$ of the electoral votes, about how many votes does it cast?

# Exploring Multiplying Fractions by Fractions

1. Are the products below the same? How can you tell?

$$0.5 \times 0.6 = 0.30$$

$$\frac{1}{2} \times \frac{3}{5} = \frac{3}{10}$$

_____

2. Are the products below the same? How can you tell?

$$0.7 \times 0.3 = 0.21$$

$$\frac{7}{10} \times \frac{3}{10} = \frac{21}{100}$$

_____

**Use the model to help you find the product. Write the product in simplest form.**

3. $\frac{2}{3} \times \frac{1}{3} =$ _____

4. $\frac{2}{5} \times \frac{1}{2} =$ _____

5. $\frac{4}{5} \times \frac{3}{4} =$ _____

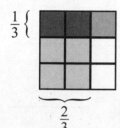

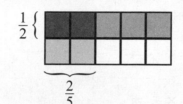

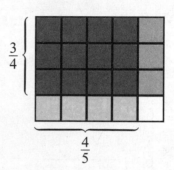

**Draw a model for each problem. Tell whether the product in *a* is the same as the product in *b*. Write *yes* or *no*.**

6. **a.** $0.5 \times 0.3 = 0.15$ _____

   **b.** $\frac{1}{2} \times \frac{3}{10} = \frac{3}{20}$

7. **a.** $\frac{3}{4} \times \frac{1}{4} = \frac{3}{16}$ _____

   **b.** $0.7 \times 0.2 = 0.14$

8. **a.** $\frac{1}{6} \times \frac{1}{5} = \frac{1}{30}$ _____

   **b.** $0.6 \times 0.2 = 0.12$

9. **a.** $0.3 \times 0.1 = 0.03$ _____

   **b.** $\frac{3}{10} \times \frac{1}{10} = \frac{3}{100}$

## NUMBER SENSE

**Write = or ≠ for each problem.**

10. $\frac{1}{2} \times \frac{1}{3} \bigcirc \frac{1}{3} \times \frac{1}{2}$

11. $\frac{1}{5} \times \frac{2}{3} \bigcirc \frac{2}{5} \times \frac{1}{3}$

12. $\frac{1}{6} \times \frac{2}{3} \bigcirc \frac{5}{6} \times \frac{1}{3}$

# More Multiplying Fractions by Fractions

**Complete the multiplication sentence. Write the product in simplest form.**

1. $\frac{2}{3} \times \dfrac{\boxed{\phantom{0}}}{\boxed{\phantom{0}}} = \dfrac{\boxed{\phantom{0}}}{\boxed{\phantom{0}}}$

2. $\frac{1}{4} \times \dfrac{\boxed{\phantom{0}}}{\boxed{\phantom{0}}} = \dfrac{\boxed{\phantom{0}}}{\boxed{\phantom{0}}}$

3. $\dfrac{\boxed{\phantom{0}}}{\boxed{\phantom{0}}} \times \frac{5}{6} = \dfrac{\boxed{\phantom{0}}}{\boxed{\phantom{0}}}$

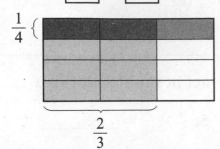

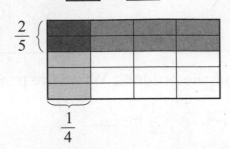

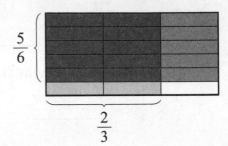

**Solve. Write the product in simplest form.**

4. $\frac{1}{4} \times \frac{1}{5} =$ _____

5. $\frac{1}{4} \times \frac{1}{4} =$ _____

6. $\frac{1}{5} \times \frac{2}{7} =$ _____

7. $\frac{1}{2} \times \frac{5}{6} =$ _____

8. $\frac{3}{8} \times \frac{1}{5} =$ _____

9. $\frac{4}{5} \times \frac{1}{10} =$ _____

10. $\frac{3}{7} \times \frac{5}{6} =$ _____

11. $\frac{5}{6} \times \frac{6}{7} =$ _____

12. $\frac{2}{5} \times \frac{4}{7} =$ _____

13. $\frac{1}{9} \times \frac{2}{3} =$ _____

14. $\frac{4}{7} \times \frac{1}{12} =$ _____

15. $\frac{5}{9} \times \frac{9}{10} =$ _____

## MIXED APPLICATIONS

16. One third of the students in Mrs. Monroe's class have pets. One half of these pets are dogs. What part of the students have a dog?

17. Spike has $\frac{2}{3}$ of a book left to read. He read $\frac{1}{4}$ of the unread part last night. What part of the entire book did he read last night?

_____

_____

## NUMBER SENSE

**Look at each set of fractions. Find the multiplication pattern. Write the next three numbers in each set.**

18. $\frac{1}{2}, \frac{1}{4}, \frac{1}{8},$ _____, _____, _____

19. $\frac{1}{3}, \frac{1}{9}, \frac{1}{27},$ _____, _____, _____

20. $\frac{3}{4}, \frac{3}{8}, \frac{3}{16},$ _____, _____, _____

21. $\frac{2}{3}, \frac{4}{9}, \frac{8}{27},$ _____, _____, _____

**112**

# Multiply Fractions Using Models

Write a fraction multiplication sentence for each model.

1.

2.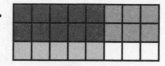

3.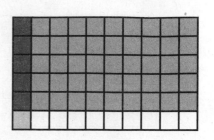

_____     _____     _____

Multiply. Write the answer in simplest form.

4. $\frac{3}{4} \times \frac{1}{2} =$ _____

5. $\frac{2}{3} \times \frac{1}{9} =$ _____

6. $\frac{2}{5} \times \frac{1}{5} =$ _____

7. $\frac{1}{5} \times \frac{1}{2} =$ _____

8. $\frac{2}{7} \times \frac{1}{4} =$ _____

9. $\frac{5}{12} \times \frac{1}{5} =$ _____

10. $\frac{1}{3} \times \frac{1}{9} =$ _____

11. $\frac{3}{10} \times \frac{3}{10} =$ _____

12. $\frac{1}{3} \times \frac{5}{12} =$ _____

13. $\frac{2}{3} \times \frac{2}{9} =$ _____

14. $\frac{1}{4} \times \frac{3}{4} =$ _____

15. $\frac{5}{7} \times \frac{1}{5} =$ _____

## MIXED APPLICATIONS

16. Of the 36 singers in the choir, $\frac{5}{6}$ are boys. How many of the singers are girls?

17. Joan has $\frac{1}{2}$ yard of felt. She will use $\frac{1}{3}$ of it to make place cards. How much felt will she use for place cards?

_____     _____

## NUMBER SENSE

18. Find the product of several pairs of fractions less than one, for example: $\frac{1}{3} \times \frac{2}{5}$. Compare the products you find to 1. Then write a rule about the product when you multiply two numbers that are less than one.

_____

_____

**113**

# More Multiplying Using Models

**Find the product. Write the answer in simplest form.**

1.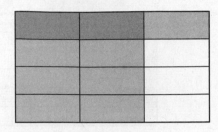

$\frac{1}{4} \times \frac{2}{3} =$ _____

2.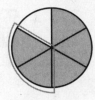

$\frac{2}{5} \times \frac{5}{6} =$ _____

**Draw a model. Find the product. Write the answer in simplest form.**

3. $\frac{4}{5} \times \frac{1}{2} =$ _____

4. $\frac{3}{4} \times \frac{1}{3} =$ _____

5. $\frac{3}{8} \times \frac{2}{3} =$ _____

6. $\frac{3}{5} \times \frac{3}{5} =$ _____

---

### MIXED APPLICATIONS

7. Nora has a piece of ribbon that is $\frac{3}{4}$ yard long. She will use $\frac{1}{2}$ of it to make a bow. What length of the ribbon will she use for the bow?

_____

8. Marlon bought $\frac{7}{8}$ pound of turkey at the deli. He used $\frac{2}{3}$ of it to make sandwiches for lunch. How much of the turkey did Marlon use for sandwiches?

_____

# Multiplying Fractions: Another Method

**Simplify the factors and rewrite the problem.**

1. $\frac{1}{3} \times \frac{3}{4}$ ___ $\frac{1}{1} \times \frac{1}{4}$ ___

2. $\frac{1}{2} \times \frac{4}{4}$ _____

3. $\frac{3}{7} \times \frac{5}{6}$ _____

4. $\frac{3}{7} \times \frac{7}{9}$ _____

5. $\frac{3}{5} \times \frac{2}{9}$ _____

6. $\frac{5}{10} \times \frac{2}{3}$ _____

7. $\frac{2}{3} \times \frac{9}{10}$ _____

8. $\frac{4}{8} \times \frac{3}{4}$ _____

9. $\frac{6}{8} \times \frac{2}{15}$ _____

10. $\frac{3}{5} \times \frac{5}{6}$ _____

11. $\frac{3}{4} \times \frac{12}{15}$ _____

12. $\frac{2}{12} \times \frac{24}{28}$ _____

**Find the product. Use any method. Write the product in simplest form.**

13. $\frac{2}{3} \times \frac{3}{4} =$ _____

14. $\frac{4}{7} \times \frac{2}{8} =$ _____

15. $\frac{3}{10} \times \frac{5}{9} =$ _____

16. $\frac{6}{7} \times \frac{14}{15} =$ _____

17. $\frac{6}{12} \times \frac{2}{3} =$ _____

18. $\frac{5}{12} \times \frac{3}{11} =$ _____

19. $\frac{3}{16} \times \frac{4}{9} =$ _____

20. $\frac{7}{24} \times \frac{6}{14} =$ _____

21. $\frac{6}{11} \times \frac{22}{24} =$ _____

22. $\frac{5}{16} \times \frac{4}{15} =$ _____

23. $\frac{6}{10} \times \frac{15}{16} =$ _____

24. $\frac{5}{9} \times \frac{12}{15} =$ _____

25. $\frac{2}{13} \times \frac{2}{16} =$ _____

26. $\frac{3}{4} \times \frac{12}{15} =$ _____

27. $\frac{5}{12} \times \frac{24}{25} =$ _____

## MIXED APPLICATIONS

28. Ashley had $\frac{3}{8}$ of a veggie pizza left after a party. She gave $\frac{1}{6}$ of the remaining pizza to Jon. What part of the entire pizza did she give Jon?

29. One-half of Mr. Sheng's shirts are white, and $\frac{2}{3}$ of his white shirts have short sleeves. What part of Mr. Sheng's shirts are short-sleeved white shirts?

_____ _____

## NUMBER SENSE

**Write the missing digit that will make each equation true.**

30. $\frac{2}{5} \times \frac{\boxed{\phantom{0}}}{2} = \frac{1}{5}$

31. $\frac{\boxed{\phantom{0}}}{3} \times \frac{9}{16} = \frac{3}{8}$

32. $\frac{8}{9} \times \frac{3}{\boxed{\phantom{0}}} = \frac{2}{3}$

# Estimating Products of Fractions

**Round to a benchmark fraction to estimate the product.**

1. $\frac{4}{5} \times \frac{2}{3} =$ _____ 2. $\frac{5}{12} \times \frac{8}{9} =$ _____ 3. $\frac{10}{11} \times \frac{4}{7} =$ _____ 4. $\frac{6}{15} \times \frac{3}{5} =$ _____

**Use compatible numbers to estimate the product.**

5. $\frac{1}{3} \times 59 =$ _____  6. $\frac{1}{6} \times 373 =$ _____

7. $710 \times \frac{2}{3} =$ _____  8. $\frac{4}{7} \times 482 =$ _____

**Tell whether the estimate is reasonable. Write _yes_ or _no_.**

9. $\frac{5}{6} \times 30 \approx 30$ _____  10. $\frac{2}{3} \times 16 \approx 10$ _____  11. $\frac{6}{11} \times 235 \approx 200$ _____

12. $\frac{1}{4} \times 405 \approx 100$ _____  13. $\frac{14}{15} \times \frac{7}{12} \approx \frac{1}{2}$ _____  14. $\frac{8}{17} \times 340 \approx 200$ _____

15. $\frac{4}{5} \times 678 \approx 750$ _____  16. $\frac{1}{3} \times 400 \approx 200$ _____  17. $\frac{3}{4} \times 807 \approx 600$ _____

18. $\frac{5}{6} \times 298 \approx 250$ _____  19. $\frac{7}{15} \times 300 \approx 100$ _____  20 $\frac{2}{3} \times 150 \approx 75$ _____

## MIXED APPLICATIONS

21. At a sporting goods store, about $\frac{3}{5}$ of the tennis rackets in stock are metal. If there are 52 tennis rackets, about how many are metal?

_____

22. Andy collects baseball hats. In his collection, $\frac{1}{3}$ of the caps are blue. If he has 42 baseball caps, how many are blue?

_____

## MIXED REVIEW

**Find the difference. Write your answer in simplest form.**

23. $2\frac{1}{2} - \frac{1}{4} =$ _____  24. $6\frac{1}{4} - 2\frac{4}{5} =$ _____

25. $7\frac{2}{5} - 3\frac{1}{2} =$ _____  26. $1\frac{2}{3} - \frac{5}{6} =$ _____

**Simplify the factors and rewrite the problem.**

27. $\frac{6}{7} \times \frac{12}{15}$ _____  28. $\frac{10}{11} \times \frac{22}{24}$ _____

Name _____ Date _____

# Multiplying Fractions and Mixed Numbers

**Write a multiplication sentence for each model.**

1. _____ × _____ = _____

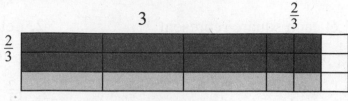

2. _____ × _____ = _____

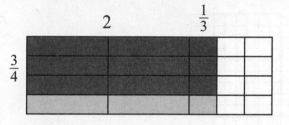

3. _____ × _____ = _____

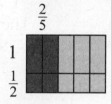

**Sketch a model to help you find each product.**

4. $\frac{1}{3} \times 2\frac{2}{3} =$ _____

5. $\frac{3}{4} \times 2\frac{1}{4} =$ _____

6. $\frac{1}{2} \times 2\frac{1}{8} =$ _____

7. $\frac{3}{4} \times 3\frac{1}{2} =$ _____

8. $\frac{2}{3} \times 1\frac{1}{2} =$ _____

9. $\frac{5}{8} \times 1\frac{1}{2} =$ _____

## MIXED APPLICATIONS

10. Chen's report will take $8\frac{1}{3}$ hours to complete. He has worked on it for $\frac{3}{5}$ of that time. How long has he worked?

11. The chickens laid $6\frac{1}{4}$ dozen eggs. The farmer sold $\frac{2}{5}$ of them. How many eggs are left?

_____

_____

## GEOGRAPHY CONNECTION

12. Badwater Basin in Death Valley, California, is the lowest point in North America. Its elevation is 282 feet below sea level. The lowest point in Europe is on the shore of the Caspian Sea. If this point is about $\frac{1}{3}$ the elevation of Death Valley, how many feet below sea level is it?

_____

**117**

# Area and Mixed Numbers

**Use the grid to find the area.**

**1.** Let each square represent
$\frac{1}{4}$ unit by $\frac{1}{4}$ unit.

$2\frac{1}{4} \times 1\frac{1}{2} =$ _____

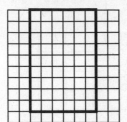

_____ squares cover the diagram.

Each square is

_____ × _____ = _____ square unit.

The area of the diagram is

_____ × $\frac{\square}{\square}$ = _____ square units.

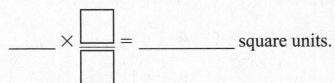

**2.** Let each square represent
$\frac{1}{3}$ unit by $\frac{1}{3}$ unit.

$1\frac{2}{3} \times 2\frac{1}{3} =$ _____

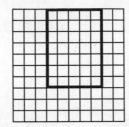

The area is _____ square units.

**3.** $1\frac{1}{8} \times 2\frac{1}{2}$          **4.** $2\frac{2}{3} \times 1\frac{1}{3}$          **5.** $1\frac{3}{4} \times 2\frac{1}{2}$

_____          _____          _____

## MIXED APPLICATIONS

**6.** Ava's bedroom rug is $2\frac{3}{4}$ feet long and $2\frac{1}{2}$ feet wide. What is the area of the rug?

**7.** A painting is $2\frac{2}{3}$ feet long and $1\frac{1}{2}$ feet high. What is the area of the painting? Use an area model to solve.

_____          _____

# Multiplying with Mixed Numbers

**Rewrite each multiplication sentence. Rename the mixed number as a fraction. Simplify the fraction.**

**1.** $1\frac{3}{4} \times \frac{4}{5}$ _____

**2.** $2\frac{6}{7} \times 3\frac{2}{3}$ _____

**3.** $2\frac{1}{3} \times 1\frac{3}{5}$ _____

**Tell whether the product will be less than both factors, between the two factors, or greater than both factors. Write: $<$, *between*, or $>$.**

**4.** $\frac{1}{6} \times \frac{4}{5}$ _____

**5.** $\frac{1}{8} \times 3\frac{1}{2}$ _____

**6.** $\frac{4}{5} \times 2\frac{1}{6}$ _____

**7.** $2\frac{5}{6} \times 3\frac{1}{7}$ _____

**8.** $2\frac{1}{7} \times 1\frac{4}{9}$ _____

**9.** $1\frac{6}{14} \times \frac{1}{10}$ _____

**10.** $\frac{4}{5} \times 1\frac{1}{2}$ _____

**11.** $5\frac{1}{3} \times 3\frac{2}{5}$ _____

**Find the product. Write the answer in simplest form.**

**12.** $4\frac{3}{4} \times 1\frac{1}{3} =$ _____

**13.** $1\frac{5}{6} \times 3\frac{1}{11} =$ _____

**14.** $4\frac{1}{2} \times 2\frac{2}{5} =$ _____

**15.** $7\frac{1}{8} \times 1\frac{2}{3} =$ _____

**16.** $3\frac{1}{6} \times 2\frac{2}{3} =$ _____

**17.** $1\frac{3}{4} \times 2\frac{4}{7} =$ _____

**18.** $10\frac{1}{3} \times 1\frac{1}{3} =$ _____

**19.** $3\frac{1}{7} \times 4\frac{9}{10} =$ _____

**20.** $3\frac{1}{5} \times 6\frac{1}{4} =$ _____

## MIXED APPLICATIONS

**21.** Mrs. Phillips has $1\frac{2}{3}$ cups of fruit. The fruit is $\frac{1}{4}$ grapes. How many cups of grapes does she have?

**22.** Ramona jogged $3\frac{3}{5}$ miles. Harold jogged $1\frac{2}{3}$ times as far as Ramona. How far did Harold jog?

_____

## NUMBER SENSE

**23.** Tom and Andrew worked together. One day Tom worked $3\frac{1}{2}$ hours in the morning and $\frac{3}{4}$ of this amount of time in the afternoon. Andrew worked $2\frac{1}{4}$ hours in the morning and $1\frac{1}{3}$ times as long in the afternoon. Who worked more hours, Tom or Andrew?

_____

**119**

# Problem Solving

| FIND UNKNOWN LENGTHS |
| --- |

1. Kamal's bedroom has an area of 120 square feet. The width of the room is $\frac{5}{6}$ the length of the room. What are the dimensions of Kamal's bedroom?

List the factor pairs for 120. Think: $\frac{5}{6}$ is close to 1, so the factors must be close in value.

_____

2. Marisol is painting on a piece of canvas that has an area of 180 square inches. The length of the painting is $1\frac{1}{4}$ times the width. What are the dimensions of the painting?

_____

3. A small plane is flying a banner in the shape of a rectangle. The area of the banner is 144 square feet. The width of the banner is $\frac{1}{4}$ the length of the banner. What are the dimensions of the banner?

_____

4. An artificial lake is in the shape of a rectangle and has an area of $\frac{9}{20}$ square mile. The width of the lake is $\frac{1}{5}$ the length of the lake. What are the dimensions of the lake?

_____

# Problem Solving

**USE MULTIPLICATION**

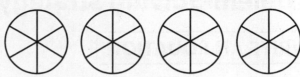

1. Sebastian bakes 4 pita breads and cuts each one into sixths. How many $\frac{1}{6}$-size slices does he have? Use the model to help you find the answer.

_____

2. Ali has 2 vegetable pizzas that she cuts into eighths. How many $\frac{1}{8}$-size pieces does she have?

_____

3. A baker has 6 loaves of bread. Each loaf weighs 1 pound. He cuts each loaf into thirds. How many $\frac{1}{3}$-pound loaves of bread does the baker now have?

_____

4. Suppose the baker has 4 loaves of bread and cuts the loaves into halves. How many $\frac{1}{2}$-pound loaves of bread would the baker have?

_____

5. Madalyn has 3 watermelons that she cuts into halves to give to her neighbors. How many neighbors will get $\frac{1}{2}$ of a watermelon?

_____

6. A landscaper had 5 tons of rock to build decorative walls. He used $\frac{1}{4}$ ton of rock for each wall. How many decorative walls did he build?

_____

# Problem-Solving Strategy

## WRITE AN EQUATION

**Write an equation. Then solve.**

1. Jane answered $\frac{3}{4}$ of the problems on a test correctly. If there were 32 problems on the test, how many did she answer correctly?

   _____

2. Carla's biscuit recipe calls for $\frac{2}{3}$ cup of flour. She wants to make $1\frac{1}{2}$ times the usual recipe. How many cups of flour will she use?

   _____

3. Mrs. Bey gave each of her grandchildren $\frac{1}{4}$ pound of grapes. If she has 9 grandchildren, how many pounds of grapes is this?

   _____

4. Wilson earns $12 an hour. He is paid $1\frac{1}{2}$ times that amount if he works on weekends. What does he earn per hour on weekends?

   _____

## MIXED APPLICATIONS

### STRATEGIES
Write a Number Sentence • Work Backward
Guess and Check

5. Arnie spent $\frac{1}{2}$ of his money at a movie, $\frac{1}{3}$ of what was left on a snack, and his last $4 on a gift. How much did Arnie spend?

   _____

6. Lana bought a total of 48 candles in 2 boxes. One box had 24 more candles than the other box. How many candles were in each box?

   _____

7. Lawrence's backpack weighs $6\frac{1}{4}$ pounds. His older brother's weighs $1\frac{5}{7}$ times as much. How much does his brother's backpack weigh?

   _____

8. Kelsey canoed on the river $5\frac{1}{2}$ miles one morning. Late that afternoon she canoed $1\frac{1}{4}$ as far as in the morning. How far did she canoe in the afternoon?

   _____

Name _____  Date _____

# Problem-Solving Applications

## MULTIPLY FRACTIONS AND MIXED NUMBERS

**Solve. Use any method.**

1. Mr. Yanaga's car has a 16-gallon gas tank. He filled the tank and then used $\frac{3}{4}$ tank on a trip. How many gallons of gas did he use?

2. One bowl of party punch uses $4\frac{3}{4}$ cups of sparkling water. How many cups of sparking water are needed to make 3 bowls of party punch?

_____

3. Terry lives $\frac{5}{8}$ mile from town. Maria lives halfway between Terry and town. How far from town does Maria live?

4. Each lap around the school track is $\frac{1}{4}$ mile. After soccer practice, the team runs 6 laps around the track. How many miles do they run?

_____

5. Kevin made five shirts. Each shirt used $\frac{2}{3}$ yard of fabric. How many yards of fabric did he use to make the shirts?

6. Will lives $\frac{9}{16}$ mile from his office. Latasha lives one third as far from her office. How far does Latasha live from her office?

_____

7. Tanisha bought $25\frac{1}{2}$ feet of wood at $4.00 a foot. How much did she pay for the wood?

8. The Thompson family's new deck is $19\frac{2}{5}$ feet long. What is the length of the deck in inches? (Remember, 12 in. = 1 ft.)

_____

**123**

# Problem Solving

## WRITE A NUMBER SENTENCE

**Write a number sentence. Then solve each problem.**

**1.** Jim has a gift-wrapping business. On average, he needs $2\frac{1}{2}$ feet of ribbon to wrap a gift. How much ribbon will he need to wrap 12 gifts?

_____

**2.** Tyrone drinks $3\frac{1}{2}$ cups of milk every day. How much milk does he drink in a week?

_____

**3.** A wading pool holds 400 gallons of water. If the pool is $\frac{5}{8}$ full, how many gallons of water are in it?

_____

**4.** The $3\frac{1}{5}$-mile long Pharr Bridge links the United States and Mexico. It is the longest bridge in the world linking two countries. During heavy traffic, there are 10 cars per mile in one lane along the entire bridge. How many cars is this?

_____

**5.** Perhaps the tallest tree ever measured, a eucalyptus in Australia, measured 459 feet. If a certain sequoia tree measures $\frac{2}{3}$ this height, how tall is the sequoia tree?

_____

**6.** Will lives $\frac{3}{4}$ mile from the library. Fay lives halfway between Will and the library. How far does Fay live from the library?

_____

**7.** Jill runs at a rate of one mile every $7\frac{1}{2}$ minutes. At this rate, how long will it take her to run $1\frac{1}{3}$ miles?

_____

**8.** Sonya is helping her teacher stack books on shelves. Each book is $1\frac{1}{4}$ inches thick. How many inches of shelf space do 8 books take up?

_____

# Divide Fractions and Whole Numbers

**Divide and check the quotient.**

**1.**

| 1 | | | 1 | | |
|---|---|---|---|---|---|
| $\frac{1}{3}$ | $\frac{1}{3}$ | $\frac{1}{3}$ | $\frac{1}{3}$ | $\frac{1}{3}$ | $\frac{1}{3}$ |

$2 \div \frac{1}{3} =$ _____ because _____ $\times \frac{1}{3} = 2.$

**2.**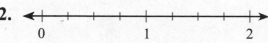

**3.**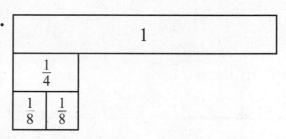

$2 \div \frac{1}{4} =$ _____ because _____ $\times \frac{1}{4} = 2.$        $\frac{1}{4} \div 2 =$ _____ because _____ $\times 2 = \frac{1}{4}.$

**Divide. Draw a number line or use fraction strips.**

**4.** $1 \div \frac{1}{5} =$ _____          **5.** $\frac{1}{6} \div 3 =$ _____          **6.** $4 \div \frac{1}{6} =$ _____

**7.** $3 \div \frac{1}{3} =$ _____          **8.** $\frac{1}{4} \div 6 =$ _____          **9.** $5 \div \frac{1}{4} =$ _____

| **MIXED APPLICATIONS** |
|---|

**10.** Amy can run $\frac{1}{10}$ mile per minute. How many minutes will it take Amy to run 3 miles?

_____

**11.** Jeremy has 3 yards of ribbon to use for wrapping gifts. He cuts the ribbon into pieces that are $\frac{1}{4}$ yard long. How many pieces of ribbon does Jeremy have?

_____

**125**

# Fraction and Whole-Number Division

**Write a related multiplication sentence to solve.**

**1.** $3 \div \frac{1}{2}$

**2.** $\frac{1}{5} \div 3$

**3.** $2 \div \frac{1}{8}$

**4.** $\frac{1}{3} \div 4$

_____     _____     _____     _____

**5.** $5 \div \frac{1}{4}$

**6.** $\frac{1}{2} \div 2$

**7.** $\frac{1}{4} \div 6$

**8.** $6 \div \frac{1}{5}$

_____     _____     _____     _____

**9.** $\frac{1}{5} \div 5$

**10.** $4 \div \frac{1}{8}$

**11.** $\frac{1}{3} \div 7$

**12.** $9 \div \frac{1}{2}$

_____     _____     _____     _____

## MIXED APPLICATIONS

**13.** Isaac has a piece of rope that is 5 yards long. Into how many $\frac{1}{2}$-yard pieces of rope can Isaac cut the rope?

_____

**14.** Two friends share $\frac{1}{2}$ of a pineapple equally. What fraction of a whole pineapple does each friend get?

_____

# Division of Fractions by Whole Numbers

**Write each reciprocal. (Hint: Two numbers are reciprocals if their product is 1.)**

**1.** 3 _____    **2.** 9 _____    **3.** 7 _____    **4.** 2 _____    **5.** 16 _____

**6.** 10 _____    **7.** 125 _____    **8.** 36 _____    **9.** 21 _____    **10.** 48 _____

**Divide by multiplying by the reciprocal. Simplify first. Then simplify the quotient if necessary.**

**11.** $\dfrac{3}{4} \div 3 = \dfrac{3}{4} \times \dfrac{1}{3} =$ _____

**12.** $\dfrac{6}{7} \div 3 = \dfrac{6}{7} \times \dfrac{1}{3} =$ _____

**13.** $\dfrac{5}{6} \div 7 = \dfrac{5}{6} \times \dfrac{1}{7} =$ _____

**14.** $\dfrac{8}{15} \div 4 = \dfrac{8}{15} \times \dfrac{1}{4} =$ _____

**Write the reciprocal. Then find the quotient in simplest form.**

**15.** $\dfrac{9}{10} \div 9 = \dfrac{9}{10} \times$ _____ $=$ _____

**16.** $\dfrac{12}{25} \div 5 = \dfrac{12}{25} \times$ _____ $=$ _____

**17.** $\dfrac{2}{3} \div 6 = \dfrac{2}{3} \times$ _____ $=$ _____

**18.** $\dfrac{4}{5} \div 10 = \dfrac{4}{5} \times$ _____ $=$ _____

**Divide. Write the quotient in simplest form.**

**19.** $\dfrac{1}{6} \div 2 =$ _____

**20.** $\dfrac{4}{6} \div 2 =$ _____

**21.** $\dfrac{11}{12} \div 7 =$ _____

**22.** $\dfrac{15}{16} \div 10 =$ _____

# Division of Mixed Numbers by Whole Numbers

**Rename the mixed number as an improper fraction. Then divide. Simplify the quotient.**

1. $3\frac{1}{2} \div 7 = \frac{7}{2} \div 7 =$ _____

2. $1\frac{2}{3} \div 5 = \frac{5}{3} \div 5 =$ _____

3. $4\frac{1}{2} \div 3 = \frac{9}{2} \div 3 =$ _____

4. $7\frac{1}{2} \div 10 = \frac{15}{2} \div 10 =$ _____

**Divide. Simplify the quotient.**

5. $3\frac{1}{7} \div 2 =$ _____

6. $4\frac{1}{8} \div 3 =$ _____

7. $3\frac{1}{3} \div 5 =$ _____

8. $5\frac{4}{7} \div 13 =$ _____

9. $6\frac{2}{3} \div 2 =$ _____

10. $2\frac{2}{3} \div 4 =$ _____

11. $3\frac{3}{4} \div 12 =$ _____

12. $1\frac{1}{3} \div 2 =$ _____

13. $3\frac{1}{9} \div 14 =$ _____

14. $4\frac{2}{5} \div 2 =$ _____

15. $8\frac{1}{4} \div 11 =$ _____

16. $2\frac{1}{4} \div 6 =$ _____

# Division of Whole Numbers by Fractions

**Rename the whole number as an improper fraction. Then divide. Simplify the quotient.**

1. $1 \div \dfrac{1}{2} = \dfrac{1}{1} \div \dfrac{1}{2} =$ _____

2. $6 \div \dfrac{3}{4} = \dfrac{6}{1} \div \dfrac{3}{4} =$ _____

3. $7 \div \dfrac{7}{8} = \dfrac{7}{1} \div \dfrac{7}{8} =$ _____

4. $14 \div \dfrac{7}{8} = \dfrac{14}{1} \div \dfrac{7}{8} =$ _____

**Divide. Simplify the quotient.**

5. $8 \div \dfrac{2}{5} =$ _____

6. $9 \div \dfrac{3}{16} =$ _____

7. $15 \div \dfrac{5}{6} =$ _____

8. $2 \div \dfrac{4}{9} =$ _____

9. $21 \div \dfrac{7}{20} =$ _____

10. $4 \div \dfrac{1}{12} =$ _____

11. $10 \div \dfrac{5}{18} =$ _____

12. $8 \div \dfrac{6}{7} =$ _____

13. $2 \div \dfrac{1}{3} =$ _____

14. $3 \div \dfrac{9}{10} =$ _____

15. $6 \div \dfrac{1}{2} =$ _____

16. $1 \div \dfrac{5}{6} =$ _____

# Interpret Division with Fractions

**Write an equation to represent the problem. Then solve.**

1. Daniel has a piece of wire that is $\frac{1}{2}$ yard long. He cuts the wire into 3 equal pieces. What fraction of a yard is each piece?

2. Vita has a piece of ribbon that is 5 meters long. She cuts the ribbon into pieces that are each $\frac{1}{3}$ meter long. How many pieces does she cut?

_____          _____

**Draw a diagram to represent the problem. Then solve.**

3. Leah has 3 oatmeal muffins. She cuts each muffin into fourths. How many $\frac{1}{4}$-muffin pieces does she have?

4. Two friends share $\frac{1}{4}$ gallon of juice equally. What fraction of the gallon of juice does each friend get?

_____          _____

5. Write a story problem to represent $3 \div \frac{1}{2}$.

_____

_____

6. Write a story problem to represent $\frac{1}{4} \div 2$.

_____

_____

**MIXED APPLICATIONS**

7. Spencer has $\frac{1}{3}$ pound of nuts. He divides the nuts equally into 4 bags. What fraction of a pound of nuts is in each bag?

8. Humma has 3 apples. She slices each apple into eighths. How many $\frac{1}{8}$-apple slices does she have?

_____          _____

Name _____  Date _____

# Problem-Solving Applications

## DIVIDE FRACTIONS AND MIXED NUMBERS

**Solve. Use any method.**

1. There are 16 cups in 1 gallon. How many cups of juice are in a container that holds $2\frac{1}{2}$ gallons of juice?

2. Anita has 20 yards of fabric to make T-shirts. Each shirt uses $\frac{3}{4}$ yard of fabric. How many T-shirts can she make?

3. The height of a bundle of shingles for a roof is 12 inches. If each shingle is $\frac{1}{4}$ inch thick, how many shingles are in the bundle?

4. A crew is paving a 22-mile road. They divided the road into $5\frac{1}{2}$-mile sections to pave each day. How many days will it take the crew to pave the whole road?

5. A truck is hauling 4 new cars that each weighs $2\frac{2}{3}$ tons. How many tons does the truck's load weigh?

6. Jeff cut a 6-foot piece of lumber into $1\frac{1}{2}$-foot pieces. How many pieces does he have?

7. A recipe for a batch of bread uses $2\frac{1}{2}$ cups of flour. Lara has a bag of flour that contains 20 cups. How many batches of bread can she make?

8. Juan has a bolt of fabric with $24\frac{1}{2}$ yards of fabric on it. He needs $3\frac{1}{2}$ yards of fabric per curtain. How many curtains can he make?

# Metric Length

The *meter* (m) is the basic metric unit of length. A *centimeter* (cm) is one hundredth of a meter. A *millimeter* (mm) is one thousandth of a meter. A *kilometer* (km) is one thousand meters.

Write a number sentence to make each conversion. Multiply to change from a larger unit to a smaller unit. Divide to change from a smaller unit to a larger unit. Use the tables to help you.

**1.** 9 m = ? cm  Think: 1 m = 100 cm

9 m × 100 cm = _____ cm

**2.** 15 m = ? km  Think: 1 m = 0.001 km

15 m × 0.001 km = _____ km

| Larger to Smaller | Smaller to Larger |
|---|---|
| 1 km = 1,000 m | 1 m = 0.001 km |
| 1 m = 100 cm | 1 cm = 0.01 m |
| 1 cm = 10 mm | 1 mm = 0.1 cm |

**Circle the better measurement.**

**3.** height of a tree

15 m   15 km

**4.** width of a rubber band

4 mm   4 m

**5.** length of a race

3 m   3 km

**6.** length of a boat

5 cm   5 m

**7.** height of a step

20 mm   20 cm

**8.** width of a bus

200 m   200 cm

**Convert each measurement to the smaller unit.**

**9.** 7 m = _____ cm

**10.** 15 cm = _____ mm

**11.** 1,200 km = _____ m

**12.** 136 km = _____ m

**13.** 84 m = _____ cm

**14.** 225 m = _____ cm = _____ mm

**Convert each measurement to the larger unit.**

**15.** 120 cm = _____ m

**16.** 4,346 m = _____ km

**17.** 890 mm = _____ cm

**18.** 750 m = _____ km

**19.** 11 cm = _____ m

**20.** 930 mm = _____ cm = _____ m

**132**

# Metric Mass

The *gram* (g) is the basic metric unit of mass. A *kilogram* (kg) is one thousand grams.

Write a number sentence to make each conversion. Multiply to change from a larger unit to a smaller unit. Divide to change from a smaller unit to a larger unit. Use the table to help you.

**1.** 3 kg = ? g  Think: 1 kg = 1,000 g

    3 kg × 1,000 g = _____ g

| | |
|---|---|
| 1 kg = 1,000 g | |
| 1 g = 0.001 kg | |

**2.** 135 g = ? kg  Think: 1 g = 0.001 kg

    135 g × 0.001 kg = _____ kg

**Circle the better measurement.**

**3.** mass of a postage stamp

    1 g   1 kg

**4.** mass of a baby

    4 g   4 kg

**5.** mass of a couch

    100 g   100 kg

**6.** mass of an orange

    500 g   500 kg

**7.** mass of a bowling ball

    5 g   5 kg

**8.** mass of an insect

    20 g   20 kg

**Convert each measurement to the smaller unit.**

**9.** 10 kg = _____ g

**10.** 4.8 kg = _____ g

**11.** 0.76 kg = _____ g

**12.** 0.004 kg = _____ g

**13.** 1.092 kg = _____ g

**14.** 305 kg = _____ g

**Convert each measurement to the larger unit.**

**15.** 2.8 g = _____ kg

**16.** 7 g = _____ kg

**17.** 3,094 g = _____ kg

**18.** 925 g = _____ kg

**19.** 52.43 g = _____ kg

**20.** 61 g = _____ kg

# Metric Capacity

The liter (L) is the basic metric unit of capacity. A milliliter (mL) is one thousandth of a liter.

Write a number sentence to make each conversion. Multiply to change from a larger unit to a smaller unit. Divide to change from a smaller unit to a larger unit. Use the table to help you.

**1.** 75 L = ? mL  Think: 1 L = 1,000 mL

    75 L × 1,000 L = _____ mL

| 1 L = 1,000 mL |
|---|
| 1 mL = 0.001 L |

**2.** 1,259 mL = ? L  Think: 1 mL = 0.001 L

    1,259 mL × 0.001 L = _____ L

**Circle the better measurement.**

**3.** capacity of a gas tank

    60 mL   60 L

**4.** capacity of cat's water bowl

    600 mL   600 L

**5.** capacity of a bathtub

    350 mL   350 L

**6.** capacity of a teacup

    300 mL   300 L

**7.** capacity of an eyedropper

    5 mL   5 L

**8.** capacity of a pitcher of iced tea

    3 mL   3 L

**Convert each measurement to the smaller unit.**

**9.** 0.7 L = _____ mL

**10.** 8 L = _____ mL

**11.** 1.6 L = _____ mL

**12.** 421 L = _____ mL

**13.** 3.09 L = _____ mL

**14.** 0.424 L = _____ mL

**Convert each measurement to the larger unit.**

**15.** 8,883 mL = _____ L

**16.** 390.7 mL = _____ L

**17.** 14 mL = _____ L

**18.** 12.5 mL = _____ L

**19.** 208 mL = _____ L

**20.** 79 mL = _____ L

# Changing Metric Units

**Complete by writing the correct unit.**

**1.** 20 kg = 20,000 _____

**2.** 3.14 m = 3,140 _____

**3.** 7.211 km = 7,211 _____

**4.** 2.091 L = 2,091 _____

**5.** 0.64 g = 640 _____

**6.** 2,981 mg = 2.981 _____

**Write *multiply* or *divide*. Then convert each measure.**

**7.** 51 L = _____ mL

**8.** 16,000 mL = _____ L

**9.** 2.1 cm = _____ mm

_____   _____   _____

**10.** 20 mm = _____ cm

**11.** 7,000 mg = _____ g

**12.** 9.21 g = _____ mg

_____   _____

---

**MIXED APPLICATIONS**

**13.** Devin has a Spanish book that has a mass of 0.65 kg. Carla has a French book that has a mass of 600 g. Whose book is lighter?

_____

**14.** If Duane adds 230 mL of milk to the 0.4 L of milk in the pitcher, how many mL of milk will be in the pitcher? How many L?

_____

---

**USE LOGICAL REASONING**

**15.** Roger, Luisa, Chin, and Tara are playing a game. For each correct answer, a game piece is moved forward. After one round, Roger's game piece has moved 15 cm. Luisa's has moved 75 mm. Chin's has moved 0.12 m. Tara's has moved 2 dm. Order the position of the students' game pieces from first to last place. (Hint: 1 dm = 0.1 m)

First  Last

_____

_____

Name _____ Date _____

# Connecting Fractions and Measurement

Use a customary ruler to measure each object to the nearest benchmark fraction:
1 inch, $\frac{1}{2}$ inch, or $\frac{1}{4}$ inch.

1.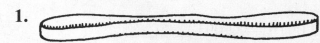

2.

_____          _____

**Name an object that measures the given length.**

3. about 3 inches long

4. about $\frac{3}{4}$ inch wide

_____          _____

## MIXED APPLICATIONS

5. Manuel made a square vegetable garden. Each side is $12\frac{1}{2}$ feet long. What is the perimeter of the garden?

6. It took Manuel 10 minutes to weed his garden, 15 minutes to fertilize it, and 20 minutes to water it. Manuel worked in his garden for what part of an hour?

_____          _____

## NUMBER SENSE

Complete the table. Estimate the length of each object. Then measure it. Find the difference between the two measures. Did you overestimate or underestimate the length?

| | Object | Estimate | Actual | Difference | Over or Under Estimate |
|---|---|---|---|---|---|
| 7. | Your little finger | | | | |
| 8. | Your math book | | | | |
| 9. | Your shoe | | | | |

Name _____  Date _____

# Customary Units

## CHANGING AND COMPUTING

**Add or Subtract.**

1.   6 ft 2 in.
   − 3 ft 5 in.

2.   4 yd 2 ft
   + 5 yd 2 ft

3.   8 yd 1 ft
   − 4 yd 4 ft

4.   3 ft 11 in.
   + 2 ft  9 in.

5.   6 ft 2 in.
   − 5 ft 3 in.

6.   3 yd 1 ft
   − 2 yd 2 ft

**Convert each measure.**

7. 2 ft = _____ in.

8. 1.5 mi = _____ yd

9. 50 yd = _____ ft

10. 48 in. = _____ ft

11. 2,640 ft = _____ yd

12. 12 ft = _____ yd

13. 5,280 yd = _____ mi

14. 108 in. = _____ yd

15. 15,840 ft = _____ mi

## MIXED APPLICATIONS

16. Yoko needs 15 feet of wood to complete a science project. She has three pieces that measure 4 ft 5 in., 5 ft 4 in., and 4 ft 11 in. Is this enough wood to finish the project?

17. Awan makes drafting tables. Each table requires one 6-foot piece of plywood. He buys plywood in 18-foot sheets. How many sheets of plywood are needed to make 75 tables?

## MIXED REVIEW

**Write the missing unit of measure.**

18. 9.404 L = 9,404 _____

19. 500 mm = 5 _____

20. 8.5 m = 850 _____

21. 5 mm = 0.005 _____

22. 3 cm = 0.03 _____

23. 9 mg = 0.009 _____

Name _____   Date _____

# Gallons, Quarts, Pints, and Cups

**Circle the better estimate.**

1.   > 1 qt   < 1 qt

2. 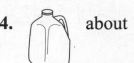  > 1 c   < 1 c

3. ![bottle] about 1 qt   about 1 gal

4. ![jug] about 1 pt   about 1 gal

**Convert each measure.**

5. 1 qt = _____ pt

6. 4 qt = _____ c

7. 2 qt = _____ pt

8. 1 gal = _____ c

9. 1 pt = _____ c

10. 6 c = _____ pt

11. 12 c = _____ qt

12. 2 gal = _____ pt

---

**MIXED APPLICATIONS**

13. A chef makes $3\frac{1}{2}$ gallons of soup to serve during lunch. If each serving is 1 cup, how many servings of soup is this?

_____

14. A biker's water bottle holds 2 quarts of water. If the biker drinks 2 cups of water, how many pints of water are left?

_____

15. One punchbowl contains 16 cups of punch. Another punchbowl contains $3\frac{1}{2}$ quarts of punch. Which punchbowl contains more punch?

_____

16. Carlton makes 5 gallons of iced mint tea. Carlton pours the tea into 40 equal-size bottles with no tea left over. How much tea is in each bottle?

_____

---

**NUMBER SENSE**

**Find the missing factor.**

17. $60 \times$ _____ $= 42,000$

18. $400 \times$ _____ $= 40$

19. $5,000 \times$ _____ $= 50$

Unit 13
Core Skills Math, Grade 5

# Changing Customary Units of Weight and Capacity

Write *multiply* or *divide*.

**1.** to change pounds to ounces

_____

**2.** to change pounds to tons

_____

**3.** to change pints to cups

_____

**4.** to change quarts to gallons

_____

**5.** to change ounces to cups

_____

**6.** to change quarts to pints

_____

**Complete. (Hint: fl oz means fluid ounce.)**

**7.** 24 qt = _____ gal

**8.** 12 qt = _____ c

**9.** 7 pt = _____ c

**10.** 4 c = _____ fl oz

**11.** 24 pt = _____ qt

**12.** $2\frac{3}{4}$ gal = _____ qt

**13.** 4 gal = _____ qt

**14.** 3 gal = _____ pt

**15.** 8 qt = _____ pt

**16.** 512 oz = _____ lb

**17.** 128 oz = _____ lb

**18.** 48 oz = _____ lb

**19.** $4\frac{1}{4}$ lb = _____ oz

**20.** 5,000 lb = _____ T

**21.** $6\frac{1}{2}$ T = _____ lb

### MIXED APPLICATIONS

**22.** The corner store has these milk prices: 1 gallon for $3.65, 1 quart for $2.29, and 1 pint for $1.19. What would be the cheapest way to buy 1 gallon of milk? Explain.

_____

**23.** During the hot summer months, Ella tries to drink 2.5 gallons of water per week. How many 8-ounce glasses of water is this per week?

_____

### NUMBER SENSE

An easy way to convert pounds to tons is to divide the number of pounds by 2, and then move the decimal point 3 places to the left. Try it.

**24.** 6,000 lb = _____ T

**25.** 4,200 lb = _____ T

**26.** 800 lb = _____ T

# Changing Units

**Read each statement. Write *true* or *false*.**

1. To change from feet to inches, multiply. _____

2. To change from miles to feet, divide. _____

3. There are 10 ounces in 1 pound. _____

4. There are 12 inches in 1 foot. _____

**Complete.**

5. 96 qt = _____ gal      6. 15 yd = _____ ft      7. 144 oz = _____ lb

## MIXED APPLICATIONS

8. Todd is making trail mix. He combines equal parts of 8 ingredients to make a $2\frac{1}{2}$-pound batch of trail mix. How many ounces of each ingredient does Todd use?

_____

9. Kyoko adds 2 ounces of nuts to every 10 ounces of fruit bar mix. If she made 5 pounds of fruit bar mix, how many ounces of nuts did she add to the mix?

_____

10. Felicia bought 2 feet of silk cord to make friendship bracelets. If she uses 8 inches of cord for each friendship bracelet, how many bracelets can she make?

_____

11. Sol has a 6-quart punchbowl. He buys 2 pints of apple juice, 2 quarts of pear juice, and 1 gallon of sparkling water. Will it all fit in the punchbowl?

_____

## NUMBER SENSE

**Complete each table. Use a calculator to check your work.**

12.

| ft | 1 | 2 | 3 | 4 | 5 |
|-----|---|---|---|---|---|
| in. | | | | | |

13.

| yd | 3 | 6 | 9 | 12 | 15 |
|-----|---|---|---|----|----|
| ft | | | | | |

14.

| gal | 1 | 2 | 3 | 4 | 5 |
|-----|---|---|---|---|---|
| pt | | | | | |

15.

| lb | 2 | 4 | 6 | 8 | 10 |
|-----|---|---|---|---|----|
| oz | | | | | |

# Customary Measurement

For Exercises 1–23, refer to the tables if necessary.

| Length |
|---|
| 1 foot (ft) = 12 inches (in.) |
| 1 yard (yd) = 3 ft = 36 in. |
| 1 mile (mi) = 1,760 yd = 5,280 ft |

| Weight |
|---|
| 1 pound (lb) = 16 ounces (oz) |
| 1 ton (T) = 2,000 lb |

| Capacity |
|---|
| 1 pint (pt) = 2 cups (c) |
| 1 quart (qt) = 2 pt |
| = 4 c |
| 1 gallon (gal) = 4 qt |
| = 8 pt |
| = 16 c |

**Convert each measurement to the larger unit.**

**1.** 39 in. = _____ ft _____ in.

**2.** 52 in. = _____ ft _____ in.

**3.** 2,500 lb = _____ T _____ lb

**4.** 35 oz = _____ lb _____ oz

**5.** 60 oz = _____ lb _____ oz

**6.** 5,550 yd = _____ mi _____ yd

**7.** 17 pt = _____ qt _____ pt

**8.** 7 c = _____ pt _____ c

**9.** 21 qt = _____ gal _____ qt

**10.** 37 ft = _____ yd _____ ft

**Convert each measurement to the smaller unit.**

**11.** 6 yd = _____ in.

**12.** 4 ft = _____ in.

**13.** 2 mi = _____ ft

**14.** 8 lb = _____ oz

**15.** 12 lb = _____ oz

**16.** 3 T = _____ lb

**17.** 7 qt 1 c = _____ c

**18.** 16 pt = _____ c

**19.** 5 gal = _____ pt

**Compare using <, >, or =.**

**20.** 12 pounds $\bigcirc$ 168 oz

**21.** 20 gal $\bigcirc$ 180 qt

**22.** 96 in. $\bigcirc$ 8 ft

**23.** 5,280 ft $\bigcirc$ 440 yd

# Exploring Volume

Each cube is 1 cubic unit. Find the volume of each figure. Use unit cubes to build the figure if it is helpful.

**1.**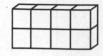

_____

**2.**

_____

**3.**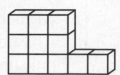

_____

**4.**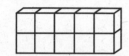

_____

**5.**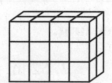

_____

**6.**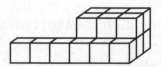

_____

**7.**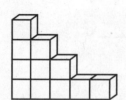

_____

**8.**

_____

**9.**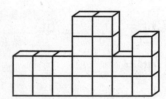

_____

---

**MIXED REVIEW**

**10.**  $\begin{array}{r} 45.7 \\ + 39.8 \\ \hline \end{array}$

**11.**  $\begin{array}{r} 6.89 \\ - 2.97 \\ \hline \end{array}$

**12.**  $\begin{array}{r} 41.09 \\ + 28.63 \\ \hline \end{array}$

**13.**  $\begin{array}{r} \$3.09 \\ - 1.98 \\ \hline \end{array}$

**14.**  $\begin{array}{r} \$16.75 \\ + 4.50 \\ \hline \end{array}$

Choose the operation. Write × or ÷.

**15.** $8 \bigcirc 0.5 = 4.0$

**16.** $7.2 \bigcirc 9 = 0.8$

**17.** $0.45 \bigcirc 0.5 = 0.9$

**18.** $60 \bigcirc 0.6 = 36$

Name _____  Date _____

# Exploring 3-Dimensional Figures

**Use what you know about hidden cubes to find the number of cubes used to build each figure.**

**1.**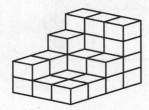

_____

**2.**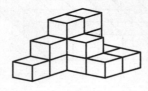

_____

**3.**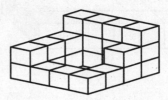

_____

**4.**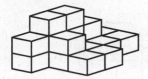

_____

**5.**

_____

**6.**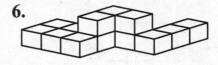

_____

**MIXED APPLICATIONS**

**7.** This top view is of which of the figures above?

_____

**8.** This is a side view of which of the figures above?

_____

**MIXED REVIEW**

**Add or subtract. Write the answers in simplest form.**

**9.** $4\frac{5}{6}$
$+ 2\frac{1}{6}$

**10.** $5\frac{4}{5}$
$- 1\frac{1}{4}$

**11.** $6\frac{1}{2}$
$+ 2\frac{3}{4}$

**12.** $10\frac{1}{4}$
$- 2\frac{3}{4}$

**13.** Explain why you multiply to convert a larger unit to a smaller unit but divide to convert a smaller unit to a larger unit. Include an example for each type of measurement conversion.

_____

Unit 14
Core Skills Math, Grade 5

# Unit Cubes and Solid Figures

**Count the number of cubes used to build each solid figure.**

1.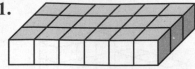

_____ unit cubes

2.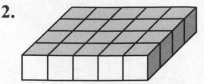

_____ unit cubes

3.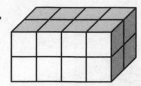

_____ unit cubes

4.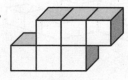

_____ unit cubes

5.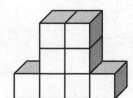

_____ unit cubes

6.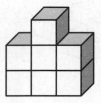

_____ unit cubes

**Compare the number of unit cubes in each solid figure. Write <, >, or =.**

7.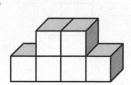

_____ unit cubes ◯ _____ unit cubes

8.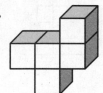

_____ unit cubes ◯ _____ unit cubes

---

**MIXED APPLICATIONS**

9. A cube-shaped carton can hold 1,000 cubes that measure 1 inch by 1 inch by 1 inch. Describe the dimensions of the carton using unit cubes.

_____

10. Peter uses unit cubes to build a figure in the shape of the letter X. What is the fewest unit cubes that Peter can use to build the figure?

_____

**144**

Unit 14
Core Skills Math, Grade 5

Name _____     Date _____

# Estimate Volume

**Estimate the volume.**

**1.** Volume of package of paper: 200 cu in.

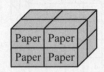

**Think:** Each package of paper has a volume of 200 cu in. There are

_____ packages of paper in the larger box. So, the volume of the

large box is about _____ × 200,

or _____ cubic inches.

Volume of large box: _____

**2.** Volume of rice box: 500 cu cm

Volume of large box: _____

**3.** Volume of tea box: 40 cu in.

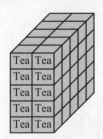

Volume of large box: _____

**4.** Volume of DVD case: 20 cu in.

Volume of large box: _____

---

## MIXED APPLICATIONS

**5.** Theo fills a large box with boxes of staples. The volume of each box of staples is 120 cu cm. Estimate the volume of the large box.

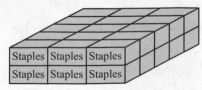

**6.** Lisa uses pudding boxes to estimate the volume of the box below. The volume of each pudding box is 150 cu in. Estimate the volume of the large box.

_____     _____

**145**

Name _____     Date _____

# Volume of Rectangular Prisms

**Find the volume.**

**1.**

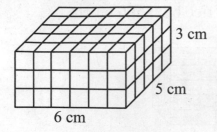

Volume: _____

**2.**

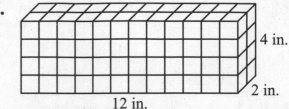

Volume: _____

**3.**

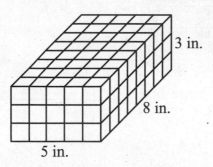

Volume: _____

**4.**

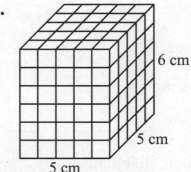

Volume: _____

**5.**

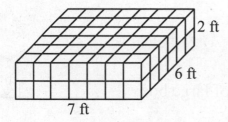

Volume: _____

**6.**

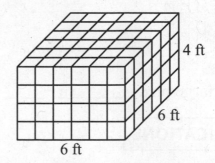

Volume: _____

## MIXED APPLICATIONS

**7.** Aaron keeps his baseball cards in a cardboard box that is 12 inches long, 8 inches wide, and 3 inches high. What is the volume of this box?

_____

**8.** Amanda's jewelry box is in the shape of a cube that has 6-inch edges. What is the volume of Amanda's jewelry box?

_____

Name _____  Date _____

# Exploring Volume

**Estimate the volume.**

1. What dimensions do you need to know to find the volume of a rectangular prism?  _____

2. How do you find the volume using these dimensions?  _____

3. Suppose the dimensions of a rectangular prism are given in inches. In what unit do you express the volume?  _____

**Tell what numbers to multiply to find the volume of each rectangular prism.**

4.

5.

6.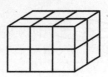

_____  _____  _____

**Find the volume.**

7.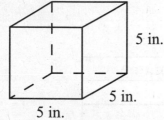
5 in.
5 in.
5 in.

8.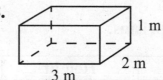
1 m
2 m
3 m

9.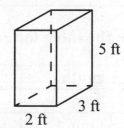
5 ft
3 ft
2 ft

_____  _____  _____

10.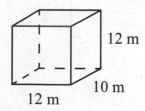
12 m
10 m
12 m

11.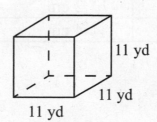
11 yd
11 yd
11 yd

12.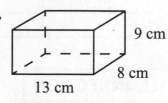
9 cm
8 cm
13 cm

_____  _____  _____

| **LOGICAL REASONING** |
|---|

13. What happens to the volume of a rectangular prism if its height is doubled and its length and width remain the same?

_____

**147**

# Volume of Rectangular Prisms

**Write a multiplication sentence to find the volume of each prism.**

**1.**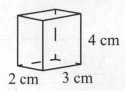
4 cm
2 cm   3 cm

_____

**2.**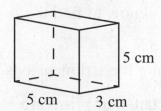
5 cm
5 cm   3 cm

_____

**3.**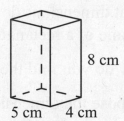
8 cm
5 cm   4 cm

_____

**4.**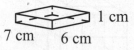
1 cm
7 cm   6 cm

_____

**5.**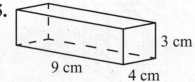
3 cm
9 cm   4 cm

_____

**6.**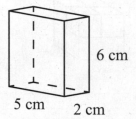
6 cm
5 cm   2 cm

_____

**Complete the table for rectangular prisms.**

|      | Length | Width | Height | Volume |
|------|--------|-------|--------|--------|
| **7.**  | 2 cm | 4 cm | 8 cm |  |
| **8.**  | 3 cm | 5 cm | 2 cm |  |
| **9.**  | 8 cm | 3 cm | 1 cm |  |
| **10.** | 4 cm |      | 2 cm | 24 cm³ |
| **11.** |      | 4 cm | 4 cm | 96 cm³ |

### MATH CONNECTION

The exponent 3 in $6^3$ means use 6 as a factor three times.

$6^3 = 6 \times 6 \times 6 = (36) \times 6 = 216.$

**Find the value.**

**12.** $2^3 =$ _____

**13.** $4^3 =$ _____

**14.** $3^3 =$ _____

**15.** $5^3 =$ _____

# More Volume of Rectangular Prisms

**Use cubes to find the number of different rectangular prisms that can be made with the given number of cubes.**

**1.** 6 cubes _____

**2.** 20 cubes _____

**Mark an X by the rectangular prism that you think has the greatest volume. Then use connecting cubes to find the volume (V) of each prism.**

**3.**

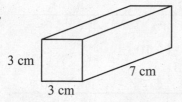

3 cm
3 cm
7 cm

V = _____ cm³

**4.**

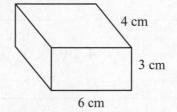

4 cm
3 cm
6 cm

V = _____ cm³

**5.**

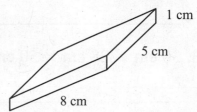

1 cm
5 cm
8 cm

V = _____ cm³

**6.**

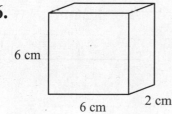

6 cm
6 cm
2 cm

V = _____ cm³

**7.**

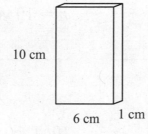

10 cm
6 cm    1 cm

V = _____ cm³

**8.**

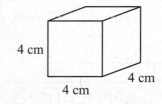

4 cm
4 cm
4 cm

V = _____ cm³

## MIXED APPLICATIONS

**9.** A swimming pool is 70 ft long and 20 ft wide and has 8 feet of water in it. What volume of water is in the pool?

_____

**10.** Felipe wants to put a 3-in. layer of mulch on an 8 ft by 10 ft garden. How many cubic feet of mulch does he need?

_____

## VISUAL THINKING

**11.** The unshaded layers show the lower part of a rectangular prism. The shaded layer is the middle of the prism. The upper layers are exactly like the lower layers. How many cubes are in the prism?

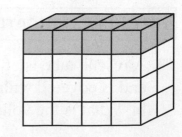

_____

Name _____ Date _____

# Applications of Volume

**Find each volume.**

1.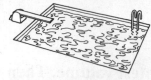

   75 ft × 25 ft × 8 ft

   _____

2.

   14 in. × 9 in. × 7 in.

   _____

3. 30 cm × 28 cm × 50 cm

   _____

4. 30 in. × 6 in. × 15 in.

   _____

5. $l$ = 7 in.
   $w$ = 8 in.
   $h$ = 5 in.

6. $l$ = 20 ft
   $w$ = 10 ft
   $h$ = 5 ft

7. $l$ = 50 yd
   $w$ = 25 yd
   $h$ = 10 yd

8. $l$ = 5.6 mm
   $w$ = 1.5 mm
   $h$ = 3.2 mm

_____   _____       _____   _____

## MIXED APPLICATIONS

9. Joe's toolbox is 20 in. long, 12 in. wide, and 10 in. high. What is the volume of his toolbox?

   _____

10. The volume of a door is 6,912 cu in. If the door is 96 in. tall and 2 in. thick, how wide is it?

    _____

11. The high school track is 400 meters long. When training, Alice usually runs 4 laps. Today she ran $\frac{3}{4}$ of her usual distance. How many meters did she run today?

    _____

12. The community swimming pool is 75 ft long. The Chois' swimming pool is $\frac{2}{3}$ that length. How long is the Chois' pool?

    _____

## PHYSICAL EDUCATION CONNECTION

13. A rescue tube is often used by lifeguards. This flotation device is made of foam cells and is covered with heavy-duty vinyl. One rescue tube measures $3\frac{1}{2}$ in. × $5\frac{1}{2}$ in. × 40 in. What is the volume of the rescue tube?

_____

**150**

# Problem–Solving Strategy

## USE A FORMULA

**Use a formula and solve.**

**1.** The swimming pool at the community center measures 50 ft by 25 ft by 5 ft. What is the volume of the pool?

_____

**2.** A dresser has 6 drawers. Each measures 5 dm by 4 dm by 2 dm. What is the maximum storage space available in the dresser?

_____

**3.** One storage bin measures 12 in. by 5 in. by 4 in. Another one measures 10 in. by 6 in. by 5 in. Which storage bin has the greater volume?

_____

**4.** Lisa packed a 12 in. by 8 in. by 4 in. box inside of a 20 in. by 15 in. by 9 in. box. How much space is left inside the larger box for packing material?

_____

## MIXED APPLICATIONS

**5.** A cube has a volume of 1,000 cm³. What is the length of its sides?

_____

**6.** The volume of a rectangular prism is 160 in.³. Its length and width are 5 in. and 2 in. What is its height?

_____

**7.** A dress pattern calls for $5\frac{3}{4}$ yd of material. Yolanda has $3\frac{1}{4}$ yd of the material she wants to use. How much more material does she need to make the dress?

_____

**8.** A box has a volume of 360 in.³. Its height is 10 in. and its length and width are whole numbers of inches. List the possible lengths and widths the box can have.

_____

## WRITER'S CORNER

**9.** Write a problem about the volume of a rectangular prism. Include the solution.

_____

_____

# Problem Solving

## VOLUME OF A RECTANGULAR PRISM

**Solve. Use the formula for the volume of a rectangular prism.**

1. A new driveway will measure 2 meters wide, 27 meters long, and 0.1 meter thick. How many cubic meters of concrete are needed for the driveway?

    _____

2. A classroom measures 14 meters by 7 meters by 3.5 meters. What is the size of the classroom in cubic meters?

    _____

3. Workers dug an 80 feet by 54 feet by 4 feet trench in the street. How much dirt was removed when they dug the hole?

    _____

4. What is the volume of a basement that measures 7 yards by 9 yards by 3 yards?

    _____

5. Tom built a storage box that is 55 centimeters by 35 centimeters by 31 centimeters. What is the volume of the storage box?

    _____

6. A water tank measures 10 feet by 12 feet by 8 feet. What is the maximum amount of water it can hold?

    _____

7. How many cubic feet of soil are needed to fill a raised vegetable bed that measures 12 feet by 10 feet by 9 inches?

    _____

8. What is the volume of a bin that measures 5 meters by 2 meters by 3.5 meters?

    _____

# Find Volume of Composed Figures

**Find the volume of the composite figure.**

**1.**

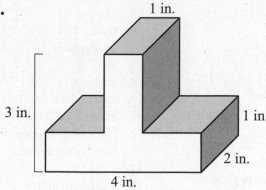

$V =$ _____

**2.**

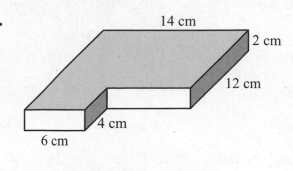

$V =$ _____

**3.**

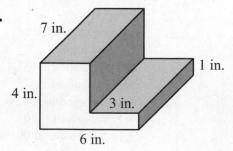

$V =$ _____

**4.**

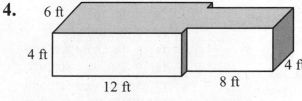

$V =$ _____

## MIXED APPLICATIONS

**5.** As part of her shop class, Jules made the figure below out of pieces of wood. How much space does the figure she made take up?

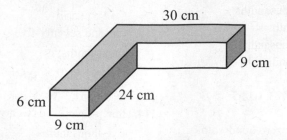

**6.** What is the volume of the composite figure below?

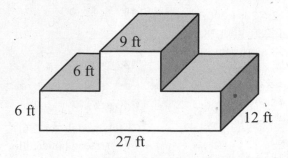

# Answer Key

## Page 1

1. 5
2. 10
3. 5
4. 100,000
5. 3
6. 1
7. 1,000
8. 4
9. 10
10. 4
11. 100
12. $10^1$
13. $10 \times 10 \times 10$
14. 10,000
15. 1,000
16. 10,000

## Page 2

1. 4,000
2. 900
3. 80
4. 50,000
5. 10; 1,000
6. 700; 70,000
7. 30; 3,000
8. 8; 800
9. 200; 20,000
10. 90; 9,000
11. 6,000; 600,000
12. 50; 5,000
13. 20 tables
14. $30,000

## Page 3

1. 6
2. 60
3. 600
4. 6,000
5. 12; 120; 1,200; 12,000
6. 4; 280; 400; 28,000
7. 58 more cans
8. 60 cans
9. $4 \times 10$
10. $4 \times 100$
11. $4 \times 1,000$

## Page 4

1. 80; 800; 8,000
2. 420; 4,200; 42,000
3. 540; 5,400; 54,000
4. 600
5. 800,000
6. 560,000
7. 480,000
8. 18,000,000
9. 4,200 times
10. 2,000 times
11. a. 7,200 times
    b. 1,800 times more
12. =
13. <
14. >
15. =

## Page 5

1. 3
2. 4
3. 1
4. 3
5. 3
6. 4; 40; 400
7. 3; 30; 300
8. 8; 80; 800
9. 7; 70; 700
10. 7; 70; 700
11. 8; 480, 80; 4,800, 800
12. 9; 450, 90; 4,500, 900
13. 5; 350, 50; 3,500, 500
14. 200 books per bookcase
15. 50 books per shelf

## Page 6

1. $12 \div 3 = 4$
2. $16 \div 2 = 8$
3. $28 \div 4 = 7$
4. $30 \div 5 = 6$
5. $n = 5$
6. $n = 2$
7. 6; 6; 60
8. 9; 9; 90
9. 4; 4; 40
10. 8; 8; 80
11. =
12. <
13. =
14. >

## Page 7

Check models for 1–6.
1. sixteen hundredths
2. five tenths
3. seventy-five hundredths
4. eight tenths
5. one and forty-two hundredths
6. one and seven hundredths
7. 0.4
8. 0.28
9. 4.86
10. 2.6
11. 0.05
12. 0.7
13. 1.5, 1.6, 1.7, 1.8
14. 2.16, 2.19, 2.25, 2.28
15. 46.45, 46.50, 46.55

## Page 8

1. one tenth
2. less than 1.0
3. It becomes one hundredth, so its value is 100 times less.
4. 0.2
5. 0.04
6. 0.003
7. 0.538
8. 63.8
9. 5.0
10. 34.7
11. 14
12. 0.02
13. 0.5
14. 0.003
15. 0.60 or 0.6
16. 0.36
17. 0.125
18. Circle: 0.35 and 0.28; 0.5, 0.07, 0.014
19. 0.014; Explanations will vary.

## Page 9

1. 3.472
2. 9.009
3. hundredths
4. thousandths
5. tenths
6. thousandths
7. hundredths
8. ones
9. 0.423, 0.095
10. a. 2
    b. zero hundredths
11. Check shading. Shapes will vary.

## Page 10

1. 6,462.203
2. 4,026.54
3. 2,001.001
4. tenths
5. tens
6. hundredths
7. ten-thousandths
8. tens; 70
9. tenths; 0.7
10. thousandths; 0.007
11. hundredths; 0.07
12. four and five tenths; four and five hundredths
13. 6,820.682
14. 4 hundred; 400
15. 7 tenths; 0.7
16. 3 thousandths; 0.003
17. 2 ones; 2

## Page 11

1. 8 hundredths; 0.08
2. 3 tenths; 0.3
3. 4 thousandths; 0.004
4. 1 tenth; 0.1
5. 6 thousandths; 0.006
6. 5 hundredths; 0.05
7. 9 hundredths; 0.09
8. 8 tenths; 0.8
9. 7 thousandths; 0.007
10. three hundred twenty-six thousandths; $(3 \times \frac{1}{10}) + (2 \times \frac{1}{100}) + (6 \times \frac{1}{1,000})$
11. eight and five hundred seventeen thousandths; $(8 \times 1) + (5 \times \frac{1}{10}) + (1 \times \frac{1}{100}) + (7 \times \frac{1}{1,000})$
12. nine hundred twenty-four thousandths; $(9 \times \frac{1}{10}) + (2 \times \frac{1}{100}) + (4 \times \frac{1}{1,000})$
13. one and seventy-five thousandths; $(1 \times 1) + (0 \times \frac{1}{10}) + (7 \times \frac{1}{100}) + (5 \times \frac{1}{1,000})$
14. thirty-seven and twenty-five thousandths
15. $(3 \times \frac{1}{10}) + (6 \times \frac{1}{100}) + (8 \times \frac{1}{1,000})$

## Page 12

1. 15.4
2. 0.55
3. 0.003
4. 6.01
5. 1.2
6. 0.018
7. 159.12
8. 708.014
9. 2 tenths; two tenths
10. 1.24; 1 and 24 hundredths
11. 0.004; four thousandths
12. 22.017; 22 and 17 thousandths
13. 18 and 27 hundredths; eighteen and twenty-seven hundredths
14. 39 and 8 hundredths
15. 231.73
16. 0.25, 0.26, 0.27, 0.28, 0.29
17. 1.11, 1.16, 1.22, 1.29, 1.37

## Page 13

1. 0.236
2. 0.971
3. 0.04
4. 0.03
5. 0.01; 1.0
6. 0.009; 0.9
7. 0.004; 0.4
8. 0.06; 6.0
9. 0.008; 0.8
10. 0.02; 2.0
11. 0.05; 5.0
12. 0.003; 0.3
13. 0.705
14. 5 thousandths, or 0.005
15. penny and quarter

## Page 14

1. 467.8; 4,678; 46,780
2. 0.456; 4.56; 45.6
3. 5.2; 52; 520
4. 0.98; 9.8; 98
5. 1.58; 0.158; 0.0158
6. 0.74; 0.074; 0.0074
7. 0.09; 0.009; 0.0009
8. 89.7; 8.97; 0.897
9. 101 mm thick
10. $0.79

11. 2,400 mL
12. 0.1007 mL

## Page 15

1. 75
2. 460
3. 0.7
4. 70
5. 6,200
6. 375
7. 0.05
8. 3.75
9. 0.0125
10. 6.4215
11. 0.0125
12. 0.26178
13. 0.7
14. 2.6178
15. 4.8
16. 0.008
17. 71,935
18. 0.375
19. 7.5
20. 3,150
21. 0.0375
22. Answers will vary. Possible answer: No. If you multiply by 10, you should get a product that is 10 times greater than 143.64. Kerry moved the decimal point one place to the left instead of one place to the right.

## Page 16

1. multiply
2. subtract
3. divide
4. subtract
5. divide
6. multiply
7. 4
8. 25
9. 20
10. 16
11. 27
12. 32
13. $6 - 2 \div 2$
14. $(2 + 4) \div 2$
15. $45 \div (9 \times 5)$
16. $7 + 1 \times 9 - 5$

Answers will vary for 17–19. Possible answers given.

17. $44 \times (4 - 4)$
18. $44 \div 4 \times 4$
19. $(44 + 4) \div 4$
20. 270 words
21. 4 million, 193 thousand, 538

## Page 17

1. 20
2. 24
3. 6
4. 84
5. 4
6. 15
7. 48
8. 7
9. $5 \times [(24 - 3) + (36 - 4)]$
10. 265 sold

## Page 18

1. 25
2. 2
3. 4
4. 7
5. 9
6. 306
7. 2.8
8. 10
9. $3 \times (8 - 5)$
10. $(20 + 12) \div (4 + 4)$
11. $(15 - 3) \div 12 + 1$
12. $(183 + 157 + 165 + 146 + 179) \div 5 = 166$ cm
13. $(5 \times 3.99) + (5 \times 2.75) + (3 \times 2.70) + (13 \times 0.89)$

## Page 19

1. 45
2. 6
3. 42
4. 5
5. 8
6. 34
7. 3
8. 27
9. 12
10. 15
11. 6
12. 32
13. 6
14. 6

15. 16
16. 25
17. 5
18. 4
19. 12
20. 567
21. 1
22. $4 \times 2 + 3^2 - 1 = 16$
23. $6 \times 3 - 3^2 = 9$
24. From the top of the triangle moving clockwise, the numbers are: 3, 8, 4, 2, 9, 5, 1, 6, 7.

## Page 20

1. >
2. <
3. >
4. <
5. <
6. >
7. <
8. >
9. <
10. <
11. >
12. >
13. 6.85
14. 0.816
15. 0.381
16. oranges
17. kiwi fruit, oranges, and potatoes
18. Like A Pro
19. Check work. Answers will vary.

## Page 21

1. >
2. >
3. >
4. >
5. <
6. <
7. >
8. <
9. <
10. <
11. >
12. <
13. <
14. <
15. <

**155**

16. .328.410
17. 4.003
18. 1.048
19. Mike; 76.9 < 78.6, so Mike took less time to run the race.
20. hundredths place; Answers will vary. Possible answer: The averages have the same digit in ones and tenths place but different digits in hundreds place. The average with the greatest digit in hundredths place is the best average.
21. Check work.

## Page 22
1. <
2. <
3. =
4. <
5. >
6. >
7. =
8. =
9. <
10. >
11. >
12. =
13. 0.3
14. 0.65
15. 3.080
16. 4.50
17. 0.789
18. 2.01
19. 0.675
20. 7.026
21. 0.034
22. 70; 700; 7,000
23. 24; 240; 2,400; 24,000
24. <
25. =
26. =
27. <

## Page 23
1. 3.7; 3.8; 4.1; 4.2; 4.4
2. 8
3. 10
4. 2
5. 1
6. 21

7. 14
8. 24
9. 53
10. 6 km
11. 13 km
12. 132,000 tickets sold; 25.5 million voters

## Page 24
1. 0.4
2. 0.5
3. 12.8
4. 46.4
5. 1,234.7
6. 4,513.8
7. 0.12
8. 0.15
9. 3.55
10. 85.61
11. 175.43
12. 78.47
13. $5.00
14. $15.00
15. $124.00
16. $57.00
17. 5
18. 12
19. 35
20. 68
21. 34.550
22. 13 dollars
23. 0.4
24. 0.7
25. 0.24
26. 1

## Page 25
1. 16 − 4
2. 4 × $3
3. 10 + 7
4. 8 ÷ 2
Check work for 5–7. Possible answers given.
5. three plus four times twelve
6. thirty-six divided by four
7. twenty-four minus six plus three
8. (30 ÷ 3) − 2
9. 30 − (3 + 2)
10. (3 × 2) × 30
11. 14 + 6
12. (25 ÷ 5) + 2

## Page 26
1. 50; 800
2. 4; 72
3. 65; 520
4. 12; 672
5. 280 mi; Rule: Multiply the map distance by 40.
6. 24 yd; Rule: Divide the number of yards of material by 2 to get the number of yards of trim.

## Page 27
1. Rule: Multiply the number of T-shirts by 3; 15, 30, 45; $45
2. Rule: Multiply the number of months by 35; 105, 140, 175, 420; $420
3. Rule: Multiply the number of stacks by 6; 60; 60 in.

## Page 28
Possible pattern given for 1–3.
1. Multiply the box number by 2 to find the number of sweaters in it; 42 sweaters
2. Add 1.5 hours to the previous time; 5:45 P.M.
3. Multiply the previous amount saved by 2; $32
4. 56 words per minute
5. 6 hr
6. Explanations will vary.

## Page 29
1. 2.8; 0.44
2. 1.03; 0.57
Check place-value charts for 3–7.
3. 23.51
4. 55.61
5. 5.4
6. 2.4
7. 5.82
8. 6.825
9. 0.603
10. 40.035
11. 0.385

## Page 30
1. 0.82

2. 24.3
3. 5.52
4. 9.32
5. 52.5
6. 6.81
7. 58.51
8. 42.38
9. 26.90
10. 26.12
11. 11.29
12. 8.05
13. 24.4
14. 56.54
15. 100.05 kg
16. 2 packages for $9.04
17. Cross out: 7.05, 7.55
18. Cross out: 90.4, 9.04, 9.2
19. Cross out: 6.3, 6.6, 60.6

## Page 31
1. 10
2. 53
3. 37
4. 300
5. 1.64
6. 4.75
7. 9.64
8. 13.13
9. 35.64
10. 53.29
11. 255.86
12. 353.01
13. 100.18
14. 2.7
15. $7.85
16. the plate lunch
17. $99.18
18. nine and eighty-four hundredths
19. 1 quarter, 2 dimes, 2 nickels, and 1 penny

## Page 32
1. 5.3
2. 3.31
3. 2.38
4. 3.64
5. 5.39
6. 16.07
7. 38.11
8. 37.77
9. 1.91
10. 8.51
11. 3.86

**156**

12. 6.5
13. 5.84
14. 22.09
15. 22.95 sec
16. 63.82 sec
17. 1.4 sec
18. 69.87 sec
19. Answers will vary.

## Page 33

1. 3
2. 4
3. 4
4. 10
5. 0.64
6. 14.59
7. $64.57
8. 0.03
9. $41.44
10. 0.16
11. 419.76
12. 10.61
13. $12.55
14. 115.07
15. 0.36
16. 0.36

## Page 34

Answers will vary for 1–4.

1. 0.80; 0.800
2. 1.3; 1.300
3. 3.00; 3.000
4. 6.40; 6.4
5. $1.20 + 4.56 = n$
6. $6.45 - 2.00 = n$
7. $8.70 - 0.02 = n$
8. $3.20 + 4.26 = n$
9. $0.43 + 0.20 = 0.63$
10. $0.80 + 0.52 = 1.32$
11. $1.42 + 0.50 = 1.92$
12. $4.00 + 23.17 = 27.17$
13. $8.10 - 5.73 = 2.37$
14. $3.86 - 0.80 = 3.06$
15. $300,000 + 4,000 + 200 + 10 + 8$
16. $30,000,000 + 4,000,000 + 500,000 + 50,000 + 6,000$
17. $\approx 1,000$
18. $\approx 220,000$
19. $\approx 8,000$
20. $\approx 24,000$

## Page 35

1. 560
2. 3,600
3. 16,000
4. 54,000
5. 40,000
6. 1,200
7. 4
8. 420
9. 3,000
10. 600
11. 8
12. 60; 600; 6,000
13. 30; 300; 3,000
14. 70; 700; 7,000
15. 50; 500; 5,000
16. 9 mi
17. Wednesday
18. Top row: 2, 7, 6;
    Middle row: 9, 5, 1;
    Bottom row: 4, 3, 8

## Page 36

1. 4,140
2. 23,256
3. 8,692
4. 24,928
5. 58,473
6. 45,212
7. 15,996
8. 34,328
9. 1,476 costumes
10. 38 dancers
11. $4,420; $4,680; $5,980; $3,744; $6,240
12. delivery person
13. $1,560 more
14. Answers will vary.

## Page 37

Estimates will vary for 1–9.

1. 8,000; 9,396
2. 15,000; 15,742
3. 120,000; 119,798
4. 720,000; 750,444
5. 1,000,000; 900,720
6. 32,000; 30,720
7. 100,000; 121,512
8. 36,000; 32,220
9. 770,000; 782,328
10. 10,500
11. 64,875
12. 23,000
13. 2,250 bulbs
14. $9.68

15. $5.04
16. $14.04
17. $12.36
18. 15,132
19. 72,600

## Page 38

1. 1,464
2. 276
3. 7,544
4. 2,079
5. 10,778
6. 12,382
7. 29,376
8. 32,565
9. 32,946
10. 27,636
11. 667
12. 17,442
13. 20,370
14. 64,186
15. 60 pairs of shoes
16. 600 players
17. 54 calories
18. 99 calories
19. 63 calories
20. 81 calories
21. 72 calories
22. 9 calories

## Page 39

Estimates will vary for 1–15.

1. 60,000
2. 350,000
3. 350,000
4. 420,000
5. 240,000
6. 216,664
7. 216,192
8. 224,190
9. 370,840
10. 82,622
11. 2,165,187
12. 1,640,688
13. 2,386,752
14. 2,478,132
15. 1,440,000
16. 13 houses
17. 39,420 meals
18. 98
19. $69.95
20. $98,765 - 10,234 = 88,531$
21. $50,123 - 49,876 = 247$

## Page 40

One possible estimate is given for 1–7.

1. 45,000
2. 3,000,000; 2,973,693
3. 12,000
4. 640,000; 658,728
5. 2,400,000; 2,280,912
6. 72,000
7. 240,000; 241,965
8. 5,168
9. 6,882
10. 98,571
11. 1,079,232
12. 1,613,465
13. 111,860
14. 1,785,848
15. 8,762,432
16. 5,130,600
17. 7,302,210
18. 256,208
19. 3,358,227
20. 448,812
21. 26,531,204
22. 97,073,208
23. about $10,000
24. 6,600 oranges
25. <
26. =
27. <

## Page 41

Check partial products for 1–4.

1. 1,786
2. 8,544
3. 7,592
4. 18,088
5. 2,166
6. 980
7. 12,644
8. 11,662
9. 4,296
10. 5,504
11. 11,077
12. 7,056
13. 7,350
14. 23,644
15. 28,880
16. 7,644
17. 25,550
18. 33,792
19. 347,655

**157**

**Page 42**

1. 693
2. 824
3. 448
4. 996
5. 848
6. 6,152
7. 4,950
8. 7,136
9. 4,347
10. 3,752
11. 6,792
12. 6,075
13. 4,460
14. 4,788
15. 2,592
16. 1,260
17. 1,120
18. 1,470
19. 1,850
20. 240
21. 1,325
22. 2,162
23. 5,220
24. 2,166
25. 448
26. 5,928
27. 5,544
28. 35,144
29. 19,470
30. 9,614

**Page 43**

1. quadrilateral; not regular
2. quadrilateral; regular
3. octagon; not regular
4. hexagon; regular
5. triangle; regular
6. pentagon; not regular

**Page 44**

1. scalene; right
2. isosceles; obtuse
3. isosceles; acute
4. scalene; right
5. scalene; obtuse
6. scalene; acute

Explanations will vary for 7–8. Possible explanation is given.

7. No. All the angles of an acute triangle measure less than 90°.

8. Yes. An equilateral triangle is also an acute triangle. Since 180° ÷ 3 = 60°, all of the angles are acute.

**Page 45**

1. triangle
2. rectangle
3. pentagon
4. octagon
5. Circle: equilateral triangle, hexagon, square, octagon
6. true
7. false
8. true
9. false
10. true
11. false
12. Check work.

**Page 46**

Check drawings for 1–4.

1. parallelogram
2. square
3. rhombus
4. trapezoid
5. Yes. A square is a special rectangle with sides that are all the same length.
6. 70 in., 140 in.
7. 25, 16, 9, 4, 1; 55 total

**Page 47**

1. parallelogram
2. rectangle
3. square
4. trapezoid
5. rhombus
6. irregular
7. irregular
8. regular
9. irregular
10. Answers will vary.
11. 2:1
12. Yes. A square is a rhombus with 4 equal angles.

13. No. It is a polygon because it is a closed figure with straight sides. It is not a quadrilateral because it has 3 sides and quadrilaterals have 4 sides.

**Page 48**

1. quadrilateral; no other classification
2. quadrilateral, parallelogram, rhombus
3. quadrilateral, parallelogram, rectangle
4. quadrilateral, parallelogram
5. quadrilateral, trapezoid
6. quadrilateral, trapezoid
7. No. If there are 3 right angles, the 4th angle must also be a right angle, so it is a rectangle.
8. True. A square has 4 right angles and 4 equal sides. This means it is a regular quadrilateral.

**Page 49**

Answers will vary for 1–3.

1. *BCEF*
2. *ABEF*
3. *ACEF, BDEF, ADEF*
4. quadrilateral, parallelogram, rhombus
5. quadrilateral, trapezoid
6. sometimes
7. always
8. never
9. sometimes
10. horizontal line parallel to base
11. diagonal line through top and bottom that does not intersect any vertex
12. vertical line that is parallel to left side and does not intersect a vertex

**Page 50**

Estimates will vary for 1–10.

1. 7
2. 10
3. 12
4. 10
5. 10
6. 5, 4 r4
7. 9, 9 r4
8. 12, 12 r2
9. 10, 10 r3
10. 11, 11 r4
11. 5 r5
12. 8 r2
13. 10 r4
14. 9 r1
15. 10 r6
16. 5 r7
17. 1 r4
18. 12
19. about 11 seats
20. 6 tickets
21. Welsh brand; 95¢ ÷ 3 is about 32¢ each.
22. 98¢ for a half dozen; 98¢ ÷ 6 ≈ 16¢ each

**Page 51**

Estimates may vary for 1–3. One possible estimate is given.

1. 40
2. 80; 82
3. 90; 89 r5
4. 77 r3
5. 79 r6
6. 153 r2
7. 124 r6
8. 156 r3
9. 22 r2
10. 23 r5
11. 107 r2
12. 84 r5
13. 59 toothpicks; 6 toothpicks
14. 182 students
15. Problems will vary.

**Page 52**

1. 16 r1
2. 12 r2
3. 23 r2
4. 53 r5

5. 48 r2
6. 124 r5
7. 85 r1
8. 74 r1
9. 76 r8
10. 157
11. 64 r4
12. 63 r1
13. 133
14. 133
15. 86 r2
16. 48 r1
17. 187 r2
18. 81 r6
19. 106 r5
20. 135 r3
21. 161 r2
22. about 50 mi
23. 154 boats
24. about 70 stamps
25. 32 books; 0 books
26. Problems will vary.

## Page 53

1. 90
2. 65 r3
3. 201 r1
4. 70 r3
5. 2,240
6. 50
7. 60
8. 80
9. 130 r2
10. 103 r5
11. 308
12. 102 r5
13. 100 r5
14. 68 r1
15. 203
16. 33 people
17. 3 boats
18. 305 paper clips
19. No. A good estimate is 700 ÷ 7 = 100, so there will be three digits in the quotient.
20. 15
21. 21
22. 53 r3
23. 66 r2
24. $9 \times 10^3$
25. $5 \times 10^2$
26. $4 \times 10^4$
27. $6 \times 10^5$

## Page 54

1. 2
2. 4
3. 9
4. 6
5. 70
6. 500
7. 2
8. 7
9. 2
10. 1
11. 30
12. 2
13. 5
14. 4
15. 40
16. 100
17. 300
18. 90
19. 100
20. 70
21. 400
22. 2,000
23. 10 seedlings
24. 12,000 drops
25. Problems will vary.

## Page 55

1. 11
2. 12
3. 15
4. 13
5. 11

Drawings may vary for 6–7.

6. 12; check drawing
7. 13; check drawing
8. 14 seats
9. 12 students

## Page 56

Check work for 1–5. Squares should be over the ones digit in the dividend.
Estimates will vary for 6–9.

6. 2; 2 r8
7. 4; 4 r8
8. 5; 5 r31
9. 5; 5 r18
10. 7; 7 r15
11. 6; 6 r20
12. 9 cartons
13. $70

14. $0.32; $0.33; $0.34; $0.37; $0.39; $0.44; $0.45

## Page 57

1. 4 r1
2. 4 r2
3. 3 r1
4. 3 r7
5. 5 r3
6. 4 r1
7. 2 r57
8. 5
9. 5 r17
10. 4 r8
11. 7 r10
12. 5 r20
13. 7
14. 6 r9
15. 9 r20
16. 6 r2
17. Answers will vary.

## Page 58

1. 2
2. 5 r23
3. 5
4. 7
5. 4 r2
6. 5
7. 7
8. 7
9. 6
10. 8 r6
11. 6 r1
12. 4
13. 8
14. 6
15. 7 r9
16. 4 r4
17. 5,936 people
18. 4 subway cars
19. Answers will vary. Possible answer: $n = 250$, $x = 5$; $n = 1,250$, $x = 25$; $n = 400$, $x = 8$; $n = 1,000$, $x = 20$; $n = 1,500$, $x = 30$; $n = 600$, $x = 12$

## Page 59

For 1–3, the square should be over the tens digit in the dividend. For 4 and 5, it should be over the ones digit.

6. 2; 2 r 11
7. 4; 3, r49
8. 4; 4 r7
9. 2; 2 r9
10. 28 r9
11. 16 r6
12. 12 r16
13. 15 r22
14. 8 bags
15. compost
16. 10-lb or 50-lb bags
17. Answers will vary.

## Page 60

1. $36
2. $6
3. $23
4. $12
5. $28
6. $29
7. $14
8. $9
9. $28
10. $23
11. 23 snapshots
12. $2,760
13. 13; 9; 18
14. 160 hr
15. $2; $4; $8; $3

## Page 61

Possible estimates given for 1–3.

1. 3
2. 2
3. 2
4. 2
5. 1 r30
6. 5
7. 3 r3
8. 1 r19
9. 2 r32
10. 3 r5
11. 2 r13
12. 6 r9
13. 1 r29
14. 1 r16
15. 9 r3
16. 2 r29

**159**

17. 5 r1
18. 2 r8
19. 3 r2
20. 4 r12
21. 2 r9
22. 3 pairs; $2 left
23. 3 trips
24. $186
25. yes
26. 7,000 hr

## Page 62

1. b
2. b
3. a
4. b
5. 7 r7
6. 3 r17
7. 5 r1
8. 6 r4
9. 5 r26
10. 6 r22
11. 3 r13
12. 3 r65
13. 7 teachers
14. 428 hours
15. 30
16. 721 r3
17. 101
18. 103 r7
19. 790 r10
20. 80; 800; 8,000
21. 120; 1,200; 12,000
22. 390; 3,900; 39,000
23. 540; 5,400; 54,000
24. 700; 7,000; 70,000

## Page 63

1. 39 r16
2. 24 r12
3. 49 r16
4. 21 r3
5. 41 r5
6. 8 r11
7. 3 r36
8. 5
9. 14 r43
10. 9 r54
11. 25 r11
12. 20 r33
13. 3 cases; 6 more spoons
14. 317 dimes
15. $396
16. 9 months

## Page 64

Estimates will vary for 1–8. One possible estimate is given.

1. 200; 246 r9
2. 300; 345 r22
3. 90; 90 r60
4. 80; 84 r24
5. 40; 41 r32
6. 60; 63 r29
7. 60; 67 r23
8. 600; 65 r14
9. 39
10. 93
11. 104
12. 78
13. 65
14. 54
15. 26
16. 46
17. 1200 ÷ 22 is about 54.5 mph, so his average speed is less than 55 mph.
18. 440 people
19. (2 × 875) + (7 × 50) = 1,750 + 350 = 2,100 ÷ 7 = 300 lb
20. 420 lb

## Page 65

1. Tony, 16 cards; Duane, 192 cards
2. Janet, 24 pages; Hallie, 240 pages
3. 44 tetras; 4 guppies
4. 248 songs

## Page 66

1. 5 hr
2. 6 boats
3. 9 tickets
4. 34 costumes
5. 4 packs
6. 40 bags; 2 muffins
7. no; 126 mi ÷ 24 mpg = 5 r6 gal used, which is less than 9 gal
8. no; 435 ÷ 36 = 12 r3. Since the division is not even, the same number of students cannot sit at each table.

## Page 67

1. Check work.
2. 6; 4
3. Move 3 units to the right and 5 units up.
4. (3, 5)

5. Answers will vary. A possible answer is given. The coordinates are sometimes called an ordered pair because the order in which you move from the origin is important. The first coordinate is a move to the right. The second is a move up.
6. (1, 3)
7. (0, 2)
8. (7, 1)
9. (5, 7)
10. Point *B*
11. Point *C*
12. Point *D*
13. Point K

## Page 68

1. (3, 1)
2. (4, 3)
3. (6, 4)
4. (2, 5)
5. (5, 6)
6. (1, 5)
7. (4, 6)
8. (8, 5)
9. Point *E*
10. Point *C*
11. Point *J*
12. Point *D*
13. *BE*
14. $3.21
15. 8 loaves
16. 6 of the 12-egg cartons and 1 of the 6-egg cartons

## Page 69

1. *X*
2. *R*
3. *C*
4. *P*
5. *U*
6. *L*
7. (8, 3)
8. (0, 4)
9. (8, 10)
10. (6, 6)
11. (2, 8)
12. (7, 9)
13. *D* (5, 0); *H* (5, 9); *B* (1, 5); *S* (4, 5)
14. Answers will vary.
15. THAT HITS THE SPOT

**160**

## Page 70

1. (2, 3)
2. (5, 7)
3. (4, 8)
4. (9, 3)
5. (3, 4)
6. (6, 5)
7–12.

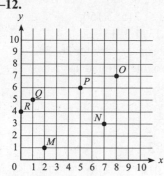

13. Price Slicer Mart
14. 6 miles

## Page 71

1. (3, 4)
2. (6, 1)
3. (4, 3)
4. (3, 5)
5. Art
6. Claire
7. Ellen
8. Denny
9. rectangle
10. $7.00
11. Check drawings.

## Page 72

1.

**Outdoor Temperature**

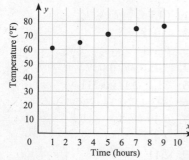

2. (1, 61); (3, 65); (5, 71); (7, 75); (9, 77)
3. Answers will vary. One possible answer is given. There would be 4 ordered pairs and the first coordinates for them would be 1, 2, 3, and 4.

4.

**Windows Repaired**

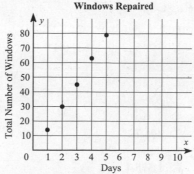

5. (1, 14); (2, 30); (3, 45); (4, 63); (5, 79)
6. Answers may vary. One possible answer is given. After 2 days, a total of 30 windows have been repaired.

## Page 73

1. (10, 8); (11, 11); (12, 16); (1, 27); (2, 31); (3, 38); (4, 41)
2. Answers may vary. One possible answer is given. Scale: 0 to 50;
3. Answers may vary. One possible answer is given. Interval: 5
4.

**Hourly Temperature**

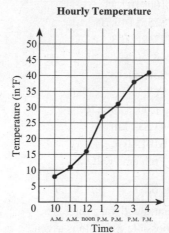

5. 16°F
6. between 10 A.M. and 11 A.M. and between 3 P.M. and 4 P.M.
7. 25°F

## Page 74

1. 3; 12

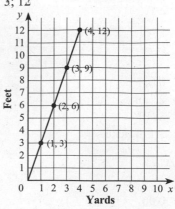

2. 4; 20

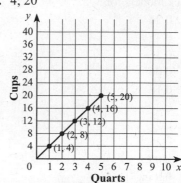

3. Answers may vary. One possible answer is given. Extend the line until it crosses the vertical line for 9 qt. From that point, draw a horizontal line to the y-axis. The number on the y-axis where the horizontal line meets is the number of cups in 9 qt.
4. 36 cups

## Page 75

Check line plots.
1. $\frac{1}{4} + \frac{1}{4} + \frac{1}{4} + \frac{1}{4}$
2. 2 lb
3. 3 lb
4. 6 lb
5. $\frac{1}{2}$ lb
6. 2 in.
7. $1\frac{7}{8}$ in.
8. 8 in.
9. $\frac{4}{7}$ in.

## Page 76

1. 1.3
2. 314
3. 42,300
4. 3; 30; 300
5. 62; 620; 6,200
6. 80.4; 804; 8,040

7. 13.1; 131; 1,310
8. 7
9. 40
10. 19.4
11. 6,510
12. 492
13. 8,033
14. 23 miles
15. $210
16. 3,170 tickets

## Page 77

1. 0.21
2. 0.06

Check models for 3–5.

3. 0.24
4. 0.45
5. 0.35
6. 0.06
7. 0.18
8. 0.2
9. 0.72
10. 0.28
11. 0.09
12. 0.8 in.

## Page 78

1. 0.18
2. 0.16
3. 0.85
4. 0.42
5. 0.4
6. 0.76
7. 0.64
8. 0.1
9. 1.04
10. 0.6 ft
11. 0.72 mi

## Page 79

1. 0.28
2. 0.81
3. 0.90
4. 1.6
5. 0.99
6. 3.55
7. 0.92
8. 1.08 mi
9. 1.35 m

## Page 80

Check models for 1–2.

1. 351.5; 270 + 63 + 15 + 3.5 = 351.5
2. 20.16
3. 6.89
4. 2,416.5
5. 406.72
6. 8.84
7. 1,375.4
8. 974.78
9. 66.22 lb
10. 31.5 mi

## Page 81

1. 36.4
2. 25.12
3. $79.69
4. $172.41
5. $431.55

Estimates will vary for 6–14.
One possible estimate is given.

6. 30; 32
7. $48; $49.24
8. 100; 107.75
9. $15; $149.70
10. 27; 26.703
11. 48; 50.4
12. $50; 54.18
13. 9; 9.306
14. 1,200; 1,300.76
15. 41.834 km
16. $101.40
17. Problems will vary.

## Page 82

Estimates will vary for 1–16.
One possible estimate is given.

1. 1; 0.98
2. 3; 2.88
3. 24; 23.31
4. 30; 29.264
5. 35; 39.644
6. 40; 40.888
7. 120; 131.12
8. 101; 114
9. 120; 121.841
10. 1,500; 1,383.21
11. 1; 1.28
12. 36; 39.06
13. 27; 25.16
14. 16; 14.595
15. 1,200; 1,059.48

16. 18; 16.614
17. >
18. >
19. =
20. <
21. 1,252.373 calories
22. 68.1 tons
23. 5.6; 56; 560
24. 31.5; 315; 3,150
25. 0.13; 1.3; 13

Estimates may vary for 26–28.
One possible estimate is given.

26. 30
27. 220
28. 65

## Page 83

1. 0.018
2. 0.04
3. 0.066
4. 0.02
5. 0.036
6. 0.092
7. 13.455
8. 6.03
9. 1
10. 0.009
11. 0.024
12. 1.51
13. 1.21
14. 0.858
15. $27.56
16. $57.45
17. 0.05, $0.41; $8.27, $0.41, $8.68

## Page 84

1. 61.7
2. 0.048
3. 0.311
4. 3.7; 0.37; 0.037
5. 21.1; 2.11; 0.211
6. 293.4; 29.34; 2.934
7. 0.39
8. 7.4
9. 2.11
10. 0.217
11. 5.13
12. 0.928
13. 0.64
14. 3.7
15. 1.27
16. 0.816
17. 10.24
18. 0.431

19. $18.25
20. $2.63
21. Check problems.

## Page 85

1. 0.3
2. 1.23
3. 0.7
4. 0.4
5. 0.3
6. 1.62
7. 0.43
8. 1.42
9. 0.13 mi
10. $1.89

## Page 86

1. 4
2. 6
3. 4
4. 8
5. 9
6. 6
7. 7
8. 2
9. 6 packages
10. 21 headbands

## Page 87

1. 1.57
2. 0.87
3. 2.06
4. 0.84
5. 1.85
6. 1.35
7. 0.7
8. 2.3
9. 1.75
10. 4.56
11. 3.68
12. 2.05
13. 1.32
14. 1.67
15. 0.34
16. 0.57
17. $1.63
18. 2 batteries; $0.22 left
19. $2.15
20. $9.87
21. Problems will vary.

## Page 88

Estimates will vary for 1–2.
One possible estimate is given.

1. $0.09
2. $3.00
3. 0.7
4. 0.4
5. 0.8
6. 0.03
7. 0.42
8. 1.05
9. 7.6
10. 1.31
11. 8.03
12. 7.4
13. 7.2
14. 13.2
15. 5.3
16. 0.012
17. 59.3
18. $3.77
19. about $0.40
20. 0.015
21. 0.06
22. 152.76
23. 0.834
24. 1.2
25. 0.098

## Page 89

1. 1
2. $1\frac{1}{2}$
3. $1\frac{2}{3}$
4. $1\frac{1}{4}$
5. $1\frac{4}{5}$
6. $1\frac{4}{6}$ or $1\frac{2}{3}$
7. 3
8. $\frac{35}{8}$
9. $\frac{7}{2}$
10. $\frac{7}{3}$
11. $\frac{39}{4}$
12. $3\frac{1}{4}, 3\frac{1}{3}, 3\frac{7}{8}$
13. $2\frac{1}{9}, 2\frac{1}{4}, 2\frac{3}{5}$
14. $1\frac{2}{3}, 1\frac{3}{5}, 1\frac{1}{5}$
15. $5\frac{4}{5}, 5\frac{3}{5}, 5\frac{1}{9}$

## Page 90

1. 4
2. 3
3. 2
4. 1
5. $1\frac{1}{12}$
6. $1\frac{1}{2}$
7. $1\frac{1}{3}$
8. $1\frac{1}{4}$
9. $1\frac{3}{8}$
10. 6
11. $1\frac{3}{4}$
12. 3
13. 16
14. $2\frac{1}{5}$
15. 2
16. $\frac{9}{2}$
17. $\frac{29}{5}$
18. $\frac{20}{3}$
19. $\frac{29}{4}$
20. $\frac{27}{10}$
21. $\frac{74}{9}$
22. $\frac{88}{5}$
23. $\frac{77}{8}$
24. $\frac{25}{6}$
25. $\frac{13}{5}$
26. $\frac{2}{6}$ or $\frac{1}{3}$
27. $\frac{5}{10}$ or $\frac{1}{2}$
28. $\frac{3}{8}$
29. $\frac{3}{5}$
30. $\frac{7}{10}$
31. $\frac{4}{7}$

## Page 91

1. 3
2. 4
3. 7
4. 29
5. 4
6. 4
7. 44
8. 9
9. $5\frac{1}{8}$
10. $2\frac{1}{3}$
11. $2\frac{7}{11}$

12. $3\frac{3}{4}$
13. $4\frac{5}{9}$
14. 9
15. $6\frac{4}{12}$ or $6\frac{1}{3}$
16. 27
17. $2\frac{9}{14}$
18. $2\frac{15}{16}$
19. $\frac{64}{7}$
20. $\frac{52}{9}$
21. $\frac{11}{4}$
22. $\frac{44}{7}$
23. $\frac{53}{11}$
24. $\frac{27}{8}$
25. $\frac{19}{10}$
26. $\frac{65}{8}$
27. $\frac{73}{11}$
28. $\frac{39}{7}$
29. $\frac{6}{5}$
30. No. $\frac{3}{4} = 3 \times \frac{4}{4} \times 4$ $= \frac{12}{16}$
31. 1.86
32. 3.5
33. 1.09
34. 0.039
35. $\frac{4}{5}$
36. $\frac{1}{4}$
37. $\frac{3}{9}$ or $\frac{1}{3}$
38. 1

## Page 92

1. $8\frac{3}{4}$ hr
2. 51 centerpieces
3. $1\frac{1}{2}$ sandwiches
4. 80 containers
5. 12 pages
6. $18\frac{1}{3}$ oz

## Page 93

1. $\frac{8}{6}$ or $1\frac{1}{3}$
2. $\frac{7}{10}$
3. $\frac{12}{8}$ or $1\frac{1}{2}$
4. $\frac{8}{3}$ or $2\frac{2}{3}$
5. $\frac{2}{5}$
6. $\frac{6}{9}$ or $\frac{2}{3}$
7. $\frac{3}{12}$ or $\frac{1}{4}$
8. $\frac{5}{3}$ or $1\frac{2}{3}$

9. $\frac{2}{3}$ of a set
10. $1\frac{1}{5}$ packs

## Page 94

1. less than
2. greater than
3. greater than
4. equal to
5. less than
6. equal to
7. more than 1/2 tsp
8. fewer hours

## Page 95

1. less than
2. equal to
3. greater than
4. greater than
5. greater than
6. less than
7. less than
8. greater than

## Page 96

1. yes
2. yes
3. no
4. no
5. yes
6. yes
7. yes
8. no
9. no
10. yes
11. yes
12. no
13. no
14. $\frac{1}{2}$
15. $\frac{1}{2}$
16. $\frac{1}{8}$
17. $\frac{7}{10}$
18. $\frac{5}{9}$
19. $\frac{5}{6}$
20. $\frac{15}{60}$ or $\frac{1}{4}$ hr
21. $\frac{50}{60}$ or $\frac{5}{6}$ min

## Page 97

1. 16
2. 10
3. 15
4. 12
5. 15

6. 6
7. 45
8. 20
9. 12
10. 90
11. 15
12. 20
13. 18
14. 30
15. 40
16. 18
17. 35
18. 8
19. $\frac{5}{6}$
20. $\frac{11}{12}$
21. $\frac{11}{12}$
22. $\frac{1}{4}$, $\frac{1}{8}$

## Page 98

1. $\frac{7}{10}$, $\frac{5}{10}$, $\frac{2}{10}$ or $\frac{1}{5}$
2. $\frac{1}{9}$, $\frac{3}{9}$, $\frac{4}{9}$
3. $\frac{5}{8}$, $\frac{2}{8}$, $\frac{7}{8}$
4. $\frac{10}{16}$, $\frac{10}{16}$, $\frac{0}{16}$ or 0
5. $\frac{1}{4}$ c still needed
6. $\frac{5}{8}$ c
7. 2, 4, 5, 8, 14, 23

## Page 99

1. 8, 3, 11
2. 10, 10, 10
3. $\frac{10}{30}$, $\frac{12}{30}$, $\frac{22}{30}$
4. $\frac{5}{8}$
5. $\frac{2}{15}$
6. $\frac{19}{30}$
7. $\frac{3}{8}$
8. $\frac{9}{10}$
9. $\frac{1}{4}$ mi
10. $\frac{7}{8}$ tsp
11. She needs $\frac{3}{8}$ yd more than she estimated.

## Page 100

1. $\frac{8}{15}$
2. $\frac{7}{10}$
3. $\frac{11}{20}$
4. $\frac{5}{6}$
5. $\frac{3}{8}$

6. $\frac{1}{4}$
7. $\frac{3}{10}$
8. $\frac{9}{20}$
9. $\frac{2}{3}$
10. $\frac{1}{20}$
11. $\frac{13}{15}$
12. $\frac{5}{8}$
13. $\frac{13}{14}$
14. $\frac{3}{8}$
15. $\frac{2}{3}$
16. $\frac{1}{2}$
17. $\frac{3}{8}$ yd more
18. $\frac{3}{8}$ ft more
19. $\frac{5}{8}$, $\frac{2}{3}$, $\frac{3}{4}$
20. $\frac{4}{9}$, $\frac{1}{2}$, $\frac{5}{6}$
21. $\frac{1}{3}$, $\frac{5}{12}$, $\frac{8}{9}$
22. 0.005, 0.050, 0.505
23. 4.123, 41.23, 41,230

## Page 101

Estimates may vary for 1–10. One possible estimate is given.

1. 7
2. 8
3. 5
4. 8
5. 6
6. 7
7. 8
8. 11
9. 6
10. 8
11. yes
12. yes
13. yes
14. no
15. yes
16. $4\frac{7}{8}$
17. $6\frac{1}{2}$
18. $7\frac{7}{8}$
19. 6
20. $4\frac{5}{6}$
21. $5\frac{7}{10}$
22. 1,500
23. 1,505
24. 896

164

**Answer Key**
*Core Skills Math*, Grade 5

25. 212
26. 50
27. 53

## Page 102

1. $7\frac{1}{2}$
2. 10
3. $7\frac{1}{2}$
4. 4
5. 16
6. $14\frac{4}{5}$
7. $7\frac{2}{3}$
8. $5\frac{8}{13}$
9. $12\frac{3}{4}$
10. $9\frac{5}{6}$
11. $10\frac{2}{5}$
12. $16\frac{8}{9}$
13. $9\frac{17}{24}$
14. $8\frac{3}{28}$
15. $7\frac{5}{6}$
16. $17\frac{11}{15}$
17. $19\frac{25}{36}$
18. $19\frac{61}{72}$
19. $5\frac{7}{8}$ ft
20. $10\frac{7}{10}$ hr
21. No. $\frac{1}{7} + \frac{4}{21} = \frac{1}{3} < 1$

## Page 103

1. $\frac{2}{3}$
2. $2\frac{4}{5}$
3. $1\frac{1}{2}$
4. $1\frac{5}{9}$
5. $2\frac{8}{11}$
6. $3\frac{3}{5}$
7. $3\frac{2}{3}$
8. $1\frac{4}{7}$
9. $4\frac{7}{8}$
10. $1\frac{2}{9}$
11. no
12. yes
13. no
14. no
15. yes

Estimates may vary for 16–20. One possible estimate is given.

16. 3; $3\frac{2}{5}$
17. 2
18. 4; $4\frac{2}{3}$
19. 1
20. 3; $3\frac{1}{4}$
21. $1\frac{1}{2}$ ft higher

## Page 104

1. no; $\frac{2}{3} > \frac{1}{3}$
2. yes; $\frac{2}{5} < \frac{4}{5}$
3. yes; $2\frac{9}{7}$
4. no
5. yes; $2\frac{7}{5}$
6. no
7. no
8. yes; $1\frac{11}{9}$
9. $2\frac{5}{5}$
10. $2\frac{8}{7}$
11. $3\frac{13}{8}$
12. $5\frac{4}{4}$
13. $6\frac{16}{13}$
14. $7\frac{17}{15}$
15. $2\frac{1}{4}$
16. $1\frac{1}{3}$
17. $1\frac{1}{2}$
18. $1\frac{1}{3}$
19. $1\frac{5}{9}$
20. $1\frac{5}{6}$
21. $5\frac{3}{7}$
22. $2\frac{1}{7}$
23. $7\frac{4}{9}$
24. $3\frac{1}{2}$
25. $3\frac{5}{6}$
26. $6\frac{2}{5}$
27. $\frac{1}{2}$ and $\frac{1}{3}$

## Page 105

Estimates may vary for 1–6. One possible estimate is given.

1. 12
2. 3
3. 10
4. 1
5. 16
6. 3
7. $\frac{1}{2}$
8. $12\frac{1}{10}$
9. $15\frac{2}{9}$
10. $1\frac{8}{9}$
11. $16\frac{3}{20}$
12. $2\frac{1}{3}$
13. $12\frac{1}{6}$
14. $\frac{5}{8}$
15. $5\frac{13}{14}$
16. $9\frac{1}{2}$
17. $1\frac{11}{12}$
18. $8\frac{1}{12}$
19. $8\frac{1}{8}$
20. $4\frac{4}{9}$
21. $14\frac{1}{18}$
22. $10\frac{1}{4}$ hr
23. $4\frac{1}{6}$ ft
24. $4\frac{1}{2}$ c

## Page 106

1. yes; To subtract fractions, they need to have a common denominator.
2. yes; $\frac{2}{3} < \frac{3}{4}$
3. no; The denominators are already the same.
4. yes; $\frac{3}{5} < \frac{4}{5}$
5. yes
6. $2\frac{2}{4}$; no
7. $5\frac{20}{35}$, $1\frac{14}{35}$; no
8. yes
9. $1\frac{10}{15}$; no
10. yes
11. $1\frac{1}{2}$
12. $1\frac{7}{12}$
13. $4\frac{3}{10}$
14. $5\frac{11}{14}$
15. $9\frac{8}{9}$
16. $3\frac{19}{20}$
17. $1\frac{17}{20}$
18. $14\frac{10}{21}$

19. $2\frac{2}{3}$
20. Check problems.

## Page 107

One possible estimate is given for 1–3.

1. 2
2. $4\frac{1}{2}$
3. $3\frac{1}{2}$
4. $5\frac{1}{2}$
5. $5\frac{5}{28}$
6. $4\frac{2}{5}$
7. $5\frac{5}{12}$
8. $6\frac{13}{14}$
9. $6\frac{8}{15}$
10. $5\frac{5}{21}$
11. $14\frac{23}{24}$
12. $10\frac{2}{3}$
13. $19\frac{23}{30}$
14. $10\frac{13}{15}$
15. $5\frac{35}{36}$
16. $3\frac{13}{14}$
17. $3\frac{5}{8}$ points
18. $1\frac{3}{4}$ lb
19. $5\frac{1}{2}$
20. $4\frac{1}{7}$

## Page 108

1. $\frac{2}{3}$
2. $\frac{1}{5}$ mi farther
3. 62 ft
4. $23\frac{9}{16}$ lb
5. $18\frac{3}{4}$ yd
6. $2\frac{1}{4}$ oz
7. $124\frac{1}{10}$ in.
8. $64\frac{7}{10}$ cm

## Page 109

1. $\frac{3}{10}$
2. $2\frac{1}{2}$ in.
3. $18\frac{1}{4}$ ft
4. $4\frac{3}{4}$ lb
5. $200\frac{2}{15}$ carat
6. $3\frac{3}{4}$ mi

7. $3\frac{1}{5}$ in.

8. $6\frac{1}{4}$-in. piece

## Page 110

1. $\frac{1}{2} \times 4 = 2$

2. $\frac{1}{4} \times 12 = 3$

3. $\frac{2}{3} \times 6 = 4$

4. 3

5. 8

6. 3

7. 9

8. 4

9. $2\frac{1}{3}$

10. $1\frac{3}{5}$

11. 7

12. $6\frac{1}{4}$

13. 4

14. $4\frac{4}{5}$

15. $2\frac{1}{4}$

16. 200 boxes

17. $168.75

18. about 30 electoral votes

## Page 111

1. yes; $0.30 = \frac{3}{10}$

2. yes; $0.21 = \frac{21}{100}$

3. $\frac{2}{9}$

4. $\frac{1}{5}$

5. $\frac{3}{5}$

Model may vary for 6–9.

6. yes

7. no

8. no

9. yes

10. =

11. =

12. ≠

## Page 112

1. $\frac{1}{4}, \frac{1}{6}$

2. $\frac{1}{4}, \frac{1}{10}$

3. $\frac{2}{3}; \frac{5}{9}$

4. $\frac{1}{20}$

5. $\frac{1}{16}$

6. $\frac{2}{35}$

7. $\frac{5}{12}$

8. $\frac{3}{40}$

9. $\frac{2}{25}$

10. $\frac{5}{14}$

11. $\frac{5}{7}$

12. $\frac{8}{35}$

13. $\frac{2}{27}$

14. $\frac{1}{21}$

15. $\frac{1}{2}$

16. $\frac{1}{6}$ of the students

17. $\frac{1}{6}$ of the entire book

18. $\frac{1}{16}, \frac{1}{32}, \frac{1}{64}$

19. $\frac{1}{81}, \frac{1}{243}, \frac{1}{729}$

20. $\frac{3}{32}, \frac{3}{64}, \frac{3}{128}$

21. $\frac{16}{81}, \frac{32}{243}, \frac{64}{729}$

## Page 113

1. $\frac{1}{2} \times \frac{1}{3} = \frac{1}{6}$

2. $\frac{5}{8} \times \frac{2}{3} = \frac{5}{12}$

3. $\frac{1}{10} \times \frac{5}{6} = \frac{5}{60}$, or $\frac{1}{12}$

4. $\frac{3}{8}$

5. $\frac{2}{27}$

6. $\frac{2}{25}$

7. $\frac{1}{10}$

8. $\frac{1}{14}$

9. $\frac{1}{12}$

10. $\frac{1}{27}$

11. $\frac{9}{100}$

12. $\frac{5}{36}$

13. $\frac{4}{27}$

14. $\frac{3}{16}$

15. $\frac{1}{7}$

16. 6 are girls.

17. $\frac{1}{6}$ yd

18. Answers may vary. One possible answer is given. When you multiply two fractions less than one, the product is less than one.

## Page 114

1. $\frac{2}{12}$ or $\frac{1}{6}$

2. $\frac{2}{6}$ or $\frac{1}{3}$

Check models for 3–6.

3. $\frac{2}{5}$

4. $\frac{1}{4}$

5. $\frac{1}{4}$

6. $\frac{9}{25}$

7. $\frac{3}{8}$ yd

8. $\frac{7}{12}$ lb

## Page 115

1. $\frac{1}{1} \times \frac{1}{4}$

2. $\frac{1}{1} \times \frac{1}{2}$

3. $\frac{1}{7} \times \frac{5}{2}$

4. $\frac{1}{1} \times \frac{1}{3}$

5. $\frac{1}{5} \times \frac{2}{3}$

6. $\frac{1}{1} \times \frac{1}{3}$

7. $\frac{1}{1} \times \frac{3}{5}$

8. $\frac{1}{8} \times \frac{3}{1}$

9. $\frac{1}{2} \times \frac{1}{5}$

10. $\frac{1}{1} \times \frac{1}{2}$

11. $\frac{1}{1} \times \frac{3}{5}$

12. $\frac{1}{1} \times \frac{1}{7}$

13. $\frac{1}{2}$

14. $\frac{1}{7}$

15. $\frac{1}{6}$

16. $\frac{4}{5}$

17. $\frac{1}{3}$

18. $\frac{5}{44}$

19. $\frac{1}{12}$

20. $\frac{1}{8}$

21. $\frac{1}{2}$

22. $\frac{1}{12}$

23. $\frac{9}{16}$

24. $\frac{4}{9}$

25. $\frac{1}{52}$

26. $\frac{3}{5}$

27. $\frac{2}{5}$

28. $\frac{1}{16}$ of the pizza

29. $\frac{1}{3}$ of the shirts

30. 1

31. 2

32. 4

## Page 116

Estimates may vary for 1–8. One possible estimate is given.

1. 1

2. $\frac{1}{2}$

3. $\frac{1}{2}$

4. $\frac{1}{4}$

5. 20

6. 60

7. 480

**Answer Key**
Core Skills Math, Grade 5

8. 280
9. yes
10. yes
11. no
12. yes
13. yes
14. no
15. no
16. no
17. yes
18. yes
19. no
20. no
21. about 30 tennis rackets
22. 14 caps
23. $2\frac{1}{4}$
24. $3\frac{9}{20}$
25. $3\frac{9}{10}$
26. $\frac{5}{6}$
27. $\frac{2}{7} \times \frac{12}{5}$
28. $\frac{5}{1} \times \frac{1}{6}$

## Page 117

1. $3\frac{2}{3} \times \frac{2}{3} = 2\frac{4}{9}$
2. $2\frac{1}{3} \times \frac{3}{4} = 1\frac{3}{4}$
3. $\frac{2}{5} \times 1\frac{1}{2} = \frac{3}{5}$

Check drawings for 4–9.

4. $\frac{8}{9}$
5. $1\frac{11}{16}$
6. $1\frac{1}{16}$
7. $2\frac{5}{8}$
8. 1
9. $\frac{15}{16}$
10. 5 hr
11. $3\frac{3}{4}$ doz or 45 eggs
12. 94 ft below sea level

## Page 118

1. $3\frac{3}{8}$; 54; $\frac{1}{4} \times \frac{1}{4} = \frac{1}{16}$; $54 \times \frac{1}{16} = \frac{54}{16}$, or $3\frac{3}{8}$
2. $3\frac{8}{9}$; $3\frac{8}{9}$
3. $2\frac{13}{16}$
4. $3\frac{5}{9}$
5. $4\frac{3}{8}$
6. $6\frac{7}{8}$ sq ft
7. 4 sq ft

## Page 119

1. $\frac{7}{1} \times \frac{1}{5}$
2. $\frac{20}{7} \times \frac{7}{3}$
3. $\frac{7}{3} \times \frac{8}{5}$
4. <
5. between
6. between
7. >
8. >
9. between
10. between
11. >
12. $6\frac{1}{3}$
13. $5\frac{2}{3}$
14. $10\frac{4}{5}$
15. $11\frac{7}{8}$
16. $8\frac{4}{9}$
17. $4\frac{1}{2}$
18. $13\frac{7}{9}$
19. $15\frac{2}{5}$
20. 20
21. $\frac{5}{12}$ c
22. 6 mi
23. Tom

## Page 120

1. 10 ft by 12 ft
2. 12 in. by 15 in.
3. 6 ft by 24 ft
4. $\frac{3}{10}$ mi by $1\frac{1}{2}$ mi

## Page 121

1. 24 pita slices
2. 16 pieces
3. 18 loaves
4. 8 loaves
5. 6 neighbors
6. 20 decorative walls

## Page 122

1. $\frac{3}{4} \times 32 = 24$ problems correct
2. $\frac{2}{3} \times 1\frac{1}{2} = 1$ cup
3. $9 \times \frac{1}{4} = 2\frac{1}{4}$ lb of grapes
4. $\$12 \times 1\frac{1}{2} = \$18$
5. $12
6. 12 candles and 36 candles
7. $10\frac{5}{7}$ lb
8. $6\frac{7}{8}$ miles

## Page 123

1. 12 gal
2. $14\frac{1}{4}$ c
3. $\frac{5}{16}$ mi
4. $1\frac{1}{2}$ mi
5. $3\frac{1}{3}$ yd
6. $\frac{3}{16}$ mi
7. $102.00
8. $232\frac{4}{5}$ in.

## Page 124

1. 30 ft
2. $24\frac{1}{2}$ c
3. 250 gal
4. 32 cars
5. 306 ft
6. $\frac{3}{8}$ mi
7. 10 min
8. 10 in.

## Page 125

1. 6, 6
2. 8, 8
3. $\frac{1}{8}$; $\frac{1}{8}$
4. 5
5. $\frac{1}{18}$
6. 24
7. 9
8. $\frac{1}{24}$
9. 20
10. 30 min
11. 12 pieces

## Page 126

1. $3 \times 2 = 6$
2. $\frac{1}{5} \times \frac{1}{3} = \frac{1}{15}$
3. $2 \times 8 = 16$
4. $\frac{1}{3} \times \frac{1}{4} = \frac{1}{12}$
5. $5 \times 4 = 20$
6. $\frac{1}{2} \times \frac{1}{2} = \frac{1}{4}$
7. $\frac{1}{4} \times \frac{1}{6} = \frac{1}{24}$
8. $6 \times 5 = 30$
9. $\frac{1}{5} \times \frac{1}{5} = \frac{1}{25}$
10. $4 \times 8 = 32$
11. $\frac{1}{3} \times \frac{1}{7} = \frac{1}{21}$
12. $9 \times 2 = 18$
13. 10 pieces
14. $\frac{1}{4}$ of the pineapple

**167**

**Page 127**

1. $\frac{1}{3}$
2. $\frac{1}{9}$
3. $\frac{1}{7}$
4. $\frac{1}{2}$
5. $\frac{1}{16}$
6. $\frac{1}{10}$
7. $\frac{1}{125}$
8. $\frac{1}{36}$
9. $\frac{1}{21}$
10. $\frac{1}{48}$
11. $\frac{1}{4}$
12. $\frac{2}{7}$
13. $\frac{5}{42}$
14. $\frac{2}{15}$
15. $\frac{1}{9}; \frac{1}{10}$
16. $\frac{1}{5}; \frac{12}{125}$
17. $\frac{1}{6}; \frac{1}{9}$
18. $\frac{1}{10}; \frac{2}{25}$
19. $\frac{1}{12}$
20. $\frac{1}{3}$
21. $\frac{11}{84}$
22. $\frac{3}{32}$

**Page 128**

1. $\frac{1}{2}$
2. $\frac{1}{3}$
3. $1\frac{1}{2}$
4. $\frac{3}{4}$
5. $1\frac{4}{7}$
6. $1\frac{3}{8}$
7. $\frac{2}{3}$
8. $\frac{3}{7}$
9. $3\frac{1}{3}$
10. $\frac{2}{3}$
11. $\frac{5}{16}$
12. $\frac{2}{3}$
13. $\frac{2}{9}$
14. $2\frac{1}{5}$
15. $\frac{3}{4}$
16. $\frac{3}{8}$

**Page 129**

1. 2
2. 8
3. 8
4. 16
5. 20
6. 48
7. 18
8. $4\frac{1}{2}$
9. 60
10. 48
11. 36
12. $9\frac{1}{3}$
13. 6
14. $3\frac{1}{3}$
15. 12
16. $1\frac{1}{5}$

**Page 130**

1. $\frac{1}{6}$ yd
2. 15 pieces
3. 12
4. $\frac{1}{8}$ gal

Check problems for 5–6.

7. $\frac{1}{12}$ lb
8. 24 slices

**Page 131**

1. 40 cups
2. 26 T-shirts
3. 48 shingles
4. 4 days
5. $10\frac{2}{3}$ tons
6. 4 pieces
7. 8 batches
8. 7 curtains

**Page 132**

1. 900
2. 0.015
3. 15 m
4. 4 mm
5. 3 km
6. 5 m
7. 20 cm
8. 200 cm
9. 700
10. 150
11. 1,200,000
12. 136,000
13. 8,400

14. 22,500; 225,000
15. 1.2
16. 4.346
17. 89
18. 0.750
19. 0.11
20. 93; 0.93

**Page 133**

1. 3,000
2. 0.135
3. 1 g
4. 4 kg
5. 100 kg
6. 500 g
7. 5 kg
8. 20 g
9. 10,000
10. 4,800
11. 760
12. 4.0 or 4
13. 1,092
14. 305,000
15. 0.0028
16. 0.007
17. 3.094
18. 0.925
19. 0.05243
20. 0.061

**Page 134**

1. 75,000
2. 1.259
3. 60 L
4. 600 mL
5. 350 L
6. 300 mL
7. 5 mL
8. 3 L
9. 700
10. 8,000
11. 1,600
12. 421,000
13. 3,090
14. 424
15. 8.883
16. 0.3907
17. 0.014
18. 0.0125
19. 0.208
20. 0.079

**Answer Key**
Core Skills Math, Grade 5

## Page 135

1. g
2. mm
3. m
4. mL
5. mg
6. g
7. multiply; 51,000
8. divide; 16
9. multiply; 21
10. divide; 2
11. divide; 7
12. multiply; 9,210
13. Carla
14. 630 mL, 0.63 L
15. Conversions may vary. One possible conversion is given. Tara (0.2 m), Roger (0.15 m), Chin (0.12 m), Luisa (0.075 m)

## Page 136

1. 3 in.
2. $2\frac{1}{2}$ in.

Answers will vary for 3–4.

5. 50 ft
6. $\frac{3}{4}$ hr

Answers will vary for 7–9.

## Page 137

1. 2 ft 9 in.
2. 10 yd 1 ft
3. 3 yd
4. 6 ft 8 in.
5. 11 in.
6. 2 ft
7. 24
8. 2,640
9. 150
10. 4
11. 880
12. 4
13. 3
14. 3
15. 3
16. no
17. 25 sheets
18. mL
19. dm
20. cm
21. m
22. m
23. g

## Page 138

1. < qt
2. > 1 c
3. about 1 qt
4. about 1 gal
5. 2
6. 16
7. 4
8. 16
9. 2
10. 3
11. 3
12. 16
13. 56 servings
14. 3 pt
15. first punchbowl
16. 1 pt or 2 c
17. 700
18. 0.1 or $\frac{1}{10}$
19. 0.01 or $\frac{1}{100}$

## Page 139

1. multiply
2. divide
3. multiply
4. divide
5. divide
6. multiply
7. 6
8. 48
9. 14
10. 32
11. 12
12. 11
13. 16
14. 24
15. 16
16. 32
17. 8
18. 3
19. 68
20. $2\frac{1}{2}$
21. 13,000
22. 1 gal for $3.65; it costs about $0.46 a pint.
23. 40 glasses per week
24. 3
25. 2.1 or $2\frac{1}{10}$
26. 0.4 or $\frac{2}{5}$

## Page 140

1. true
2. false
3. false
4. true
5. 24
6. 45
7. 9
8. 5 oz of each ingredient
9. 16 oz or 1 lb of nuts
10. 3 bracelets
11. no
12. 12, 24, 36, 48, 60
13. 9, 18, 27, 36, 45
14. 8, 16, 24, 32, 40
15. 32, 64, 96, 128, 160

## Page 141

1. 3 ft 3 in.
2. 4 ft 4 in.
3. 1 T 500 lb
4. 2 lb 3 oz
5. 3 lb 12 oz
6. 3 mi 270 yd
7. 8 qt 1 pt
8. 3 pt 1 c
9. 5 gal 1 qt
10. 12 yd 1 ft
11. 216 in.
12. 48 in.
13. 10,560 ft
14. 128 oz
15. 192 oz
16. 6,000 lb
17. 29 c
18. 32 c
19. 40 pt
20. >
21. <
22. =
23. >

## Page 142

1. 8
2. 12
3. 11
4. 10
5. 24
6. 18
7. 11
8. 3
9. 19
10. 85.5
11. 3.92

## 169

12. 69.72
13. $1.11
14. $21.25
15. ×
16. ÷
17. ÷
18. ×

## Page 143

1. 27
2. 14
3. 24
4. 18
5. 12
6. 14
7. 3
8. 2, 4, 5
9. 7
10. $4\frac{11}{20}$
11. $9\frac{1}{4}$
12. $7\frac{1}{2}$
13. Answers may vary. Possible answer is given. A larger unit is made up of many smaller units. Since multiplication increases a number, you multiply. 4 ft × 12 in. per ft = 48 in. A number of small units can be grouped together to make a larger unit. You divide to find the number of groups. 12 qt ÷ 4 qt per gal = 3 gal.

## Page 144

1. 18
2. 20
3. 16
4. 6
5. 8
6. 7
7. 6 > 4
8. 5 = 5
9. 10 in. by 10 in. by 10 in.
10. 5 unit cubes

## Page 145

1. 8; 8; 1,600; 1,600 cu in.
2. 12,000 cu cm
3. 2,000 cu in.
4. 960 cu in.
5. 3,600 cu cm
6. 6,000 cu in.

## Page 146

1. 90 cm$^3$
2. 96 in.$^3$
3. 84 ft$^3$
4. 150 cm$^3$
5. 120 in.$^3$
6. 144 ft$^3$
7. 288 in.$^3$
8. 216 in.$^3$

## Page 147

1. length, width, height
2. multiply the dimensions
3. cubic inches, cu in., or in.$^3$
4. 2 × 2 × 2
5. 3 × 2 × 3
6. 2 × 3 × 2
7. 125 in.$^3$
8. 6 m$^3$
9. 30 ft$^3$
10. 1,440 m$^3$
11. 1,331 yd$^3$
12. 936 cm$^3$
13. The volume is doubled.

## Page 148

1. 2 cm × 3 cm × 4 cm = 24 cm$^3$
2. 5 cm × 3 cm × 5 cm = 75 cm$^3$
3. 4 cm × 5 cm × 8 cm = 160 cm$^3$
4. 6 cm × 7 cm × 1 cm = 42 cm$^3$
5. 4 cm × 9 cm × 3 cm = 108 cm$^3$
6. 5 cm × 2 cm × 6 cm = 60 cm$^3$
7. 64 cm$^3$
8. 30 cm$^3$
9. 24 cm$^3$
10. 3 cm
11. 6 cm
12. 8
13. 64
14. 27
15. 125

## Page 149

1. 2 possible
2. 4 possible
3. 63 cm$^3$
4. 72 cm$^3$
5. 40 cm$^3$
6. 72 cm$^3$
7. 60 cm$^3$
8. 64 cm$^3$
9. 11,200 cubic feet
10. 20 cubic feet
11. 56 cubes

## Page 150

1. 15,000 ft$^3$
2. 882 in.$^3$
3. 42,000 cm$^3$
4. 2,700 in.$^3$
5. 280 in.$^3$
6. 1,000 ft$^3$
7. 12,500 yd$^3$
8. 26.88 mm$^3$
9. 2,400 in.$^3$
10. 36 in.
11. 1,200 m
12. 50 ft
13. 770 in.$^3$

## Page 151

1. 6,250 cu ft
2. 240 cu dm
3. the second storage bin
4. 2,316 cu in.
5. 10 cm
6. 16 in.
7. $2\frac{1}{2}$ yd
8. 1 in. by 36 in.; 2 in. by 18 in.; 3 in. by 12 in.; 4 in. by 9 in.; 6 in. by 6 in.
9. Check problems.

## Page 152

1. 5.4 m$^3$
2. 343 m$^3$
3. 17,280 ft$^3$
4. 189 yd$^3$
5. 59,675 cm$^3$
6. 960 ft$^3$
7. 90 ft$^3$
8. 35 m$^3$

## Page 153

1. 12 cu in.
2. 384 cu cm
3. 105 cu in.
4. 416 cu ft
5. 2,916 cu cm
6. 2,592 cu ft

Answer Key
Core Skills Math, Grade 5